PRAISE F

In her warm, gentle, and refreshing way, Sonya helps turn her readers' focus away from troubles and heartache toward a big God who loves beyond measure. Her forty messages are filled with promise and truth—important reminders of who God is and what He's able to do. Thank you, Sonya, for this beautiful, spirit-soothing book!

Twila Belk
Writer, speaker, and author of *The Power to Be: Be Still, Be Grateful, Be Strong, Be Courageous*

It is rare to see a devotional written with such a specific focus, but that is exactly what you will find in Sonya's new work, *Whispers of God's Love: Forty Days of Hope-Filled Messages to Lift the Troubled Soul*. The book is indeed filled with hope for those who are traveling the dark path of deep trials and suffering. Sonya returns again and again to the trustworthiness of God's character, to His tender love, and to the deep purposes that He weaves through everything we experience. Her daily format includes God's character, His promises, our prayerful response and worship, and then practical things that can be done to apply the devotional. Sonya's devotional is a Scripture-soaked resource that is carefully designed for those who need it most. May God use it to minister help and healing to all who read it!

Dr. Steve Jones
President of the Missionary Church denomination, Fort Wayne, Indiana

When you need to be reminded that the Lord will carry your burdens, or when you need to take your eyes off your circumstances to place them on Christ, Sonya's devotional is where you need to turn. Her words are a declaration of the heavenly Father's compassion, love, and power. Purchase *Whispers of God's Love* today so you can begin to let God soak you in His love.

Melanie Chitwood
Writing coach and editor for Next Step Coaching Services
Author of *What a Husband Needs from His Wife* and *What a Wife Needs from Her Husband*
Former Proverbs 31 Ministries speaker and writer

Deformed living often develops out of one's distorted view of God. In this devotional material Sonya focuses upon giving clarity to the nature of God as He reveals Himself in His names and His biblical revelation. She moves beyond simply informing us about God by challenging us to respond to who God is by worshiping and reflecting upon Him. A person's journey through this book will likely cause them to deepen their relationship to the God who impacts all our lives.

Reverend Robert Reid
Pastor at large at Lancaster Bible College, Lancaster, Pennsylvania
Pastor emeritus of Calvary Monument Bible Church, Paradise, Pennsylvania

Oh, the times I've wished God would speak aloud to my hurting heart! Reading *Whispers of God's Love*, I experienced God's comfort, direction, and encouragement through choice scriptures, beloved hymn lyrics, and the tender words of Sonya. How sweet the relief, the joy, the assurance that God knows my situation and whispers His love to me through this precious book. This is a book to read again and again—and a gift for every occasion.

Nancy Sebastian Meyer Kuch
Author of *Spiritually Single Moms* and *Beyond Expectations*

Sonya writes as one who has experienced the troubling of her own soul. During those painful moments, she experienced the seasons of refreshing that flow from the heart of the Lord. His whispers, captured on these pages, will minister deeply to your soul—words of life bringing hope and healing. May you be drawn, as I was, to His abiding, comforting presence.

Dave Hess
Pastor of Christ Community Church, Camp Hill, Pennsylvania

Sonya dips deeply into the well of her own pain and struggle where God met her with His provision, strength, and comfort. Her un-sugar-coated transparency provides a rich source of encouragement for any of us who find ourselves in a season of challenge in which the voice of God may seem distant. Sonya leads readers through forty days of Scripture, prayer, and reflection, reminding us of what she found—that God's love is ever present when we learn to listen to His whisper.

Dr. Peter W. Teague
President of Lancaster Bible College, Capital Seminary and Graduate School, Lancaster, Pennsylvania

Tender, Holy Spirit driven. This book leads me to the heart of God.

Barb Simpson
Spiritual director and senior warden of Pittsburgh Diocese, Anglican Church of North America, Pittsburgh, Pennsylvania

Sonya's book beautifully combines deep spiritual truths with the very real struggles of life. She offers honesty and hope in a practical and easy-to-read format. *Whispers of God's Love* oozes with Scripture and applies it like a salve to our deepest pain. Thank you, Sonya, for sharing your heart so openly and directing your readers to our greatest source of comfort and help.

M. Esther Lovejoy
Author of *The Sweet Side of Suffering* and contributing author to *Inspired by Tozer*

Whispers of
GOD'S LOVE

Whispers of
God's Love

Forty Days of Hope-Filled Messages
to Lift the Troubled Soul

Sonya Grace Naugle

Published by Sonya Grace Naugle
Fleetwood, Pennsylvania, USA
Printed in the USA

All Scripture quotations are from the Holy Bible,
New King James Version, © 1979, 1980, 1982 by Thomas Nelson, Inc.
Used by permission. All rights reserved.

© 2019 Sonya Grace Naugle
All rights reserved

ISBN-13: 978-1-7330763-0-2

Cover and interior design by InsideOut CreativeArts

To read more from Sonya Grace Naugle,
visit her website at sonyagracenaugle.com.

Dedication

I dedicate *Whispers of God's Love* to my dear dad, whose life struggles and storms helped influence me to persevere in the writing of this book. He and I experienced many difficulties, both together and apart, but through them all our God has been faithful. God's love has healed so many of our heartaches and continues to bring me hope.

Even through the last year of his battle with cancer, Dad encouraged me to keep writing. I am forever grateful for all his support as well as the many valuable lessons I learned through journeying the winding and troubling roads of life with him. Although he did not have the opportunity to witness the completion of this book, since the Lord took him home in March 2017, I want to thank him for being my cheerleader, prayer warrior, and friend who taught me in his dying days how to truly live. Seeing my uncompleted manuscript on his desk, handled and highlighted with care, during his last weeks here on Earth gave me the motivation to keep writing when I felt like giving up. Thank you, Dad, for inspiring me to press forward in completing this assignment. Your legacy and love live on!

Contents

Dedication	9
Preface	13
Acknowledgments	17
Introduction: A Journey Worth the Struggle	21
1. I AM	27
2. I Am Your Shepherd	31
3. I Am God Most High	35
4. I Am the Everlasting God	39
5. I Am Your Peace	43
6. I Am the One Who Sees	47
7. I Am Your Sanctifier	51
8. I Am Your Healer	55
9. I Am Your All-Sufficient One	61
10. I Am Your Banner	65
11. I Am Your Provider	71
12. I Am Your Constant Companion	77
13. I Am Your Lord Almighty	83
14. I Am Your Righteousness	89
15. I Am Your Master	95
16. I Am the One True God	99
17. I Am Your Sanctuary	105
18. I Am Your Strength	111
19. I Am Your Creator	115
20. I Am Your Rock	119

21. I Am Your Forgiving Father	123
22. I Am Your Light	127
23. I Am Your Refuge	133
24. I Am Your Redeemer	137
25. I Am Your Sun and Shield	143
26. I Am Your Confidence	149
27. I Am Your Dwelling Place	155
28. I Am Your Hope	159
29. I Am Your Portion	163
30. I Am Your Song	169
31. I Am Your Deliverer	175
32. I Am the God Who Hears You	181
33. I Am Your Father of Glory	185
34. I Am the Maker of All Things	191
35. I Am the Lord Your God	197
36. I Am Your Faithful Father	201
37. I Am Your Potter	207
38. I Am He Who Is Able	213
39. I Am Your Exceedingly Great Reward	219
40. I Am Your King of Glory	225
In My Grip	231
About the Author	233
Appendix: Pronunciation Guide and Meanings for the Names of God	235
Notes	237
Selected Bibliography	239

Preface

When people fail you, plans unravel, and the cares within your soul consume you, where do you turn? Life often unfolds in ways we least expect or hope, and in our ensuing moments of grief and pain, we too often fail to run to the only One who can help and comfort us. If you need a fresh reminder of our Father's tender love and compassion, this book is for you.

Writing *Whispers of God's Love* has been a journey for me like no other. God's call to me to write this devotional came five years ago, during a time when I was at my lowest. After a tumultuous childhood followed by many years of emotionally and physically taxing cares as a pastor's wife, mom of four, and long-distance caregiver for my parents, I collapsed and became almost totally incapacitated for nine months. During this season I was forced to give up much-loved responsibilities and brought face to face with a multitude of thoughts—hurts from the past, anxieties regarding the present, and fears about the future. But in my discouragement, God began to speak quietly to my heart, slowly bringing truth, healing, and hope to my weary soul. As He did, I began to write what I heard in the pages of my journal. This book is the result.

The adversities of life can leave us feeling alone, abandoned, and forgotten. In these times, however, we have a God who promises to be with us. Fully trustworthy, He will see us through. The God of the Bible is the God of today. If we learn to listen for His voice, we will gain a better understanding of His love—a love that says, "I will never leave you nor forsake you" (Heb. 13:5); a love that says, "I am with you, My child, through the darkest night, just as I am with you on the brightest day." That's what this forty-day devotional is about: it is an invitation for you to sit for a while and listen for the Father's voice in the midst of your daily circumstances and pressing needs.

Each entry is divided into five sections: The first is a word from God to His child on some aspect of who He is. This section teaches many of God's Old Testament names and their meanings. I chose to keep these names in their original Hebrew form in order to unveil God's character and speak of His watchful eye, tender care, and supernatural touch, which can grace our most pain-filled moments with hope. This section is not a statement of my own thoughts but rather truths from God's Word that came alive to my heart during my own season of great trial. Many of the scriptures I drew from are paraphrased, while others are actual quotes and are in quotation marks. The Scripture references for all verses, whether paraphrased or quoted, are at the bottom of this section. Second, "God's Promises" contains several truths from Scripture to encourage our hearts. Third, "My Prayer" is an opportunity to ask God to make His name and promises real in our lives; the Scripture references for verses paraphrased in the prayers are listed at the bottom of this section. Fourth, "My Worship" includes a hymn to help lift our hearts to God in trust and praise. And finally, "Reflection and Realignment" gives a chance to think about all that God has revealed in the day's reading and apply the truth of who He is to our personal situations.

I pray that *Whispers of God's Love*, written from the perspective of God the Father speaking to His child, will restore hope to your heart and lift your troubled soul in the midst of life's trying times.

PREFACE

Dear heavenly Father, bless the men and women who read this book. Let its message be a great source of encouragement to them through their life struggles. Pour out Your Spirit upon them, oh God, that they may encounter a fresh revelation of Your love, and enable them to see with new eyes Your care and concern for them even on their darkest days. Resurrect a heavenly hope and a supernatural strength within their hearts and souls that will lift them above the challenges and adversities they are encountering. For Your love bears all things, believes all things, hopes all thing, endures all things—and never fails. Shine forth Your extravagant love into their hearts today, Lord God, that they may experience You in a deeper, richer way and be revived!

Acknowledgments

I am extremely blessed to be surrounded by some incredibly godly and talented people. When the Lord prompted me to write this book, I wasn't sure how it would get published. But I am so very grateful for the guidance of the Holy Spirit, who led me each step of the way.

Initially, as a member of COMPEL Training, a division of Proverbs 31 Ministries that offers online classes to encourage and instruct those who have a God-given call to write, I received helpful tools to enhance my writing. I also received the boost and encouragement I needed to step out in faith to start blogging and writing for publication.

Later, in February 2016, the Holy Spirit prompted me to attend the Writer to Writer conference in Hershey, Pennsylvania. There the Lord inspired me through the conference founders, Shawn and Suzanne, as well as Deb of Elk Lake Publishing, who encouraged me regarding my writing and affirmed that I should move forward. The insights of several Christian authors and editors also played a significant role in encouraging me to complete this book.

Thank you, Becky, for being not only my editor and proofreader but also my personal friend. This book would not have been the same without your special touch, as you have tenderly reviewed every sentence for the right words, grammar, and punctuation. I owe you a particular debt of gratitude for digging deep to help me with the Hebrew equivalents of the names of God as well as their pronunciations. Thank you too for all the time and effort you put into perfecting my writing with your skill, making it the best it could be for publication and for its readers. Also, you have helped guide me and provide me with the connections and network to bring this book to publication. Thank you to Steve too for his advice, insight, and direction regarding both publishing and marketing.

I want to thank Rob for his beautiful design work on the cover and interior of this book. I am also grateful to Jennifer for her thorough and careful proofreading of the manuscript. Both of you played a big role in making this book ready for others to see, and I greatly appreciate all your hard work.

My deepest thanks go to each of the endorsers of this book. Thank you for taking the time to read this devotional and provide me with your gracious feedback and loving support. I am so very grateful for each one of you and the investment you made in these pages.

I owe a great debt of gratitude to my precious family and friends, who stood by me, supported me, and interceded for me during this long and arduous journey.

Thank you, John and Sherry, for staying by my side and helping me through all the ups and downs as I initially labored over the text. Your willingness to share your gifts and talents with me as well as offer your listening ears, wisdom, and godly advice helped mold me as a writer and also as a woman of God. I am forever grateful!

Thank you, Sharon and Iris, for your eyes for detail and ongoing encouragement that often gave me a much-needed lift. Thank you too for your willingness to provide me with beneficial feedback about the content of this book and areas where it could be enhanced.

Acknowledgments

Thank you, Joy, Lisa, Meg, Doris, and Gals of Grace, for praying me through my setbacks and for your encouragement along the way. Your friendships have been a refreshing presence and have brought out the best in me as "iron sharpens iron" (Prov. 27:17).

Thank you, my beloved brother, Lenny, for being the best brother ever! You always know what to say to give me a boost—as well as a good laugh! Thank you too for challenging me to persevere with my writing, no matter the obstacles that came, and for inspiring me with your courage as you pursued your own dreams.

Thank you, my dear, darling husband, Nathanael. Your dedication and devotion have not only given me wings to fly but also to finish this book. You and our four children, Rachel, Benjamin, Samuel, and Susanna, never complained but rose to the occasion, continually cheering me on and believing the best of me.

Thank you, Momma G. and Mom and Dad N. and my extended family and church family, for your patience and for supporting me during this long journey with your ongoing prayers that helped sustain me through many hours of writing and rewriting.

Lastly, thank You, heavenly Father, for giving me the vision, ability, and inspiration to write and complete this book during some of the most difficult years of my adult life. Please use my feeble and fallible attempts in writing this book to bring great encouragement to Your children and great glory, honor, and praise to Your holy name.

*I*NTRODUCTION

A Journey Worth the Struggle

It was on a Sunday morning at church that I knew something was severely wrong.

As a pastor's wife and homeschooling mother of four children aged ten to sixteen, I had many responsibilities at church and at home—sitting on committees, attending meetings, mentoring women, managing my household, speaking to groups, coaching volleyball. I was also traveling 130 miles back and forth to care for my parents, with my mom living in a group home and my dad battling stage 4 colon cancer. All this was taking a toll on my marriage and family. Still, I carried on. I had always been one to take care of others' needs.

I began experiencing heart palpitations accompanied by dizziness, fatigue, sleep disturbances, digestive issues, joint and abdominal pain, muscle weakness, lower than normal blood pressure, and the inability to get over a head cold. Unfortunately, I kept going—homeschooling, coaching, serving at church, taking occasional speaking engagements, and traveling three hours each way to care for my parents.

The Sunday before Thanksgiving 2013 I went to church as usual. Strangely, I had no strength to stand up for the singing or even to sing while sitting down. During the message my heart felt as if it was doing flips in my chest. My oldest daughter, sitting next to me, saw my face turn pale and my breathing grow faster and heavier. Suddenly my limbs went limp, and everything went blank.

My juggling act had come to a screeching halt.

An ambulance rushed me to the emergency room. My blood was drawn, and I had an EKG, but the tests revealed nothing serious. After receiving an IV for dehydration, I was sent home with directions to follow up with my primary care physician and cardiologist. I didn't know it, but it would be months before I could easily get out of bed.

In the days following my collapse, I visited my primary care doctor and cardiologist. Neither of them could provide me with answers. Something was obviously wrong in my body, but I had no diagnosis or treatment plan to follow.

Days dragged into weeks. Finally, about a month after my body's breakdown, I saw a thread of God's grace. I visited a healthcare practitioner who read between the lines of my lab work to see some definite health concerns. After a few more weeks of waiting for further test results, my practitioner confirmed that I was dealing with the onset of severe adrenal fatigue, or "adrenal burnout," as she called it. This was most likely the result of many years of high-stress situations that had started in my early childhood.

I now had a diagnosis. But I had no solution.

Heart palpitations led to continual dizziness. I was incredibly weak and always tired. My limbs felt like dead weight—I had to physically pick up my legs, one at a time, and put them over the edge of the bed to try to get up. My healthcare practitioner told me that my condition was serious and that it would take a long time to recover—not months but years. The odds of me fully recovering were slim. I felt frustrated and hopeless.

At first I felt as if I was being punished. I had always tried to eat well, exercise, and keep healthy and strong. But that hadn't stopped my body from crashing.

In our performance-based world, lying in bed isn't considered resourceful. But I couldn't get up, let alone brush my hair and teeth, make meals for my family, or wash clothes. All that took energy I didn't have. My body had basically said, "I'm done."

Two months into my recovery, I held onto my various responsibilities from a distance, expecting to be back on my feet soon and able to return to my ministry roles. But after weeks of struggling, it became obvious that it wasn't going to happen. Finally I realized that I needed to surrender everything. My oldest daughter took on household responsibilities and cared for her siblings, while others filled the voids I had left on church and para-church committees. If God wanted to resurrect any of it, He could, but I had to give it all up first.

As I lay in bed with nothing to do, my mind worked overtime. Hurts from the past that I thought had been resolved and emotions that I had buried now came uncovered. With full force they bowled me over with shame, sadness, anger, fear, and resentment. I also worried about the present—how my sixteen-year-old daughter would maintain household responsibilities, how my children would be homeschooled, how shopping and meal prep would be accomplished, how my parents' pressing medical needs would be cared for, how my inability to function might create misunderstanding in those closest to me and make it appear as if I were lazy or unmotivated. Fears about the future haunted me as well: how would we pay for the supplements, treatments, and tests I now required? What would happen to my parents as they faced their own health struggles? And worst of all, would I ever be able to care for my family again?

In this place of despair, God ministered to my heart in a way I had never experienced before. While the exhaustion told me I was finished, God told me, "You're staying in this bed until you learn what I want to teach you, because I need your full attention." I was sidelined, but God was just getting started. I didn't know it, but God was going to use this season to revive my soul and body from many chaotic years and toxic experiences.

As I lay in bed, I began to fill the pages of my journal. Writing was difficult, since having lights on or sitting up in bed increased my dizziness. But I prayed, "God, if You want me to write, You'll give me the strength to hold this pen and sit up." And He did just that.

As I learned to listen for His voice, God taught me some unexpected lessons. Relying on the Holy Spirit for guidance, I wrote down what I heard God saying to my heart as I prayed through my affliction and meditated on His Word. As I looked at my struggles in light of who God is and the relationship I have with Him as one of His children, I experienced His presence in surprising new ways. Though my circumstances didn't change for many months, *I* began to change, and I found great treasures in the darkness.

Grappling with worry, shame, rejection, and fear taught me some powerful truths. First, I learned above all else that God's presence was with me. I was not alone! I would get through this. Knowing that God loved me as His own precious child brought me peace. I also discovered that God's promises are true and trustworthy, even when I didn't feel them. I had to lean into His promises and take them as my own—and I did. Amazingly, as I grew in trust, I saw God's provision—our expenses were somehow paid, my children's homeschooling carried on, my family had meals on the table and all their daily needs met, and my parents survived their struggles as they learned to trust God and lean on each other.

INTRODUCTION

My trial wasn't over in a moment—it lasted many months, and its residual effects still continue today. But those months in bed weren't wasted time; in them God was at work, healing my body, soul, and spirit and drawing me closer to Him. My trial was not a punishment but rather a present from the Lord: it slowed me down and gave me the solitude I needed to draw closer to Him. As I focused on the Lord, He spoke new life to my soul. Not only that, but He also gave me a new purpose, including the call to write books and to blog that He had planted in my heart many years previously. It was extremely difficult for me to be patient with the process and give myself permission to be still, but it was well worth it.

God had a plan in my pain, and He has a plan in yours as well. Press into Him and His promises. He can turn your pain into praise.

DAY 1

I AM

My child, I know that life doesn't make sense right now. You are caught in waves of doubt and confusion as you struggle with being set aside from your usual usefulness. In this imposed stillness, your mind is flooded with thoughts of hurts from the past and fears about the future. You sense My voice and feel prompted to write—yet you can barely hold a pen. In your helplessness, please know that I AM. I am everything you ever need and so much more. You are doubting because you have not yet discovered the depths of My love for you. My love contains the fullness of who I am—and who I am contains all the resources to help you through each and every day. Lean on Me, and let Me do the task through you.

When I say that I AM, I am saying that My presence is with you and that it is sure and empowering. When I say that I AM, I am saying that My resources are available to you and that they are secure and unlimited. I am fully aware of your need, and I am fully available to help you and sustain you through this time. As you experience moments of weakness, look to Me, for I am your strength.

Just as I was with Moses, so I am with you. I called Moses to go before Pharaoh to bring My people, the children of Israel, out of Egypt. But the challenge held him in captivity as he questioned his ability. He didn't see himself as capable for the task, and he wasn't, but I was—and I AM! When Moses questioned Me,

I reminded him that My presence was with him and that it was all he needed. My presence provides you too with the divine enabling to accomplish any task. Where Moses lacked, My power increased, and My provisions were plentiful. For I AM WHO I AM, *Yahweh*, the Lord God, and there is no other God like Me.

My child, don't weigh your ability against any assignment I have given you. Your human resources will never match up to the call. When all hope is lost, remember that I am your hope. I want to accomplish through you so much more than what your mind can humanly conceive. This is how the world will come to know Me—when they see you, by faith, attempting to do things that only I can do through you. When they see these things occurring that cannot be explained except that I, the great I AM, have accomplished them, then they will come to know and experience Me.

Like the certainty of the rising and setting of the sun, so My presence is certainly with you. My provisions for you are more than enough, and My resources will never end. So rest in Me, and receive from Me. I AM WHO I AM.

Exodus 3:14–15; Psalm 139:7–10; 2 Peter 1:3; Psalm 54:4; Isaiah 40:28–31; John 14:12; Exodus 33:14; Jeremiah 32:17

God's Promises

Moses said to God, "Who am I that I should go to Pharaoh, and that I should bring the children of Israel out of Egypt?" So He said, "I will certainly be with you...." And God said to Moses, "I AM WHO I AM." And He said, "Thus you shall say to the children of Israel, 'I AM has sent me to you.'" (Exod. 3:11–14)

He said to me, "My grace is sufficient for you, for My strength is made perfect in weakness." Therefore most gladly I will rather boast in my infirmities, that the power of Christ may rest upon me. (2 Cor. 12:9)

Ah, Lord God! Behold, You have made the heavens and the earth by Your great power and outstretched arm. There is nothing too hard for You. (Jer. 32:17)

My Prayer

Father God, the great I AM, thank You for Your eternal and fully accessible presence and provision. Without You I can do nothing, but according to Your Word, I can do all things through Christ who strengthens me. Forgive me, Lord, for weighing my frail human abilities and limited supply of strength against the tasks to which You have called me. It is evident that my strengths do not match up to Your calling because they are not meant to. Your divine assignments are meant to be matched only with Your divine resources. So I call upon You now to help me, Lord, and in faith I receive Your divine enabling so that I can do what You have called me to do. I am just a weak vessel in Your hands, but Your Word says that Your strength is made perfect in weakness. So I choose now to thank You, Lord, for my weaknesses so that Your power can be manifested through me. Thank You for being my great I AM. You are with me, You are for me, and You are able! In Jesus' name I pray. Amen.

Philippians 4:13; 2 Corinthians 12:9

My Worship

Praise to the Lord, the Almighty, the King of creation!
O my soul, praise Him, for He is thy health and salvation!
All ye who hear, now to His temple draw near;
Praise Him in glad adoration!

Praise to the Lord, who o'er all things so wondrously reigneth,
Shelters thee under His wings, yea, so gently sustaineth!
Hast thou not seen how thy desires e'er have been
Granted in what He ordaineth?

Praise to the Lord, who doth prosper thy work and defend thee;
Surely His goodness and mercy here daily attend thee.
Ponder anew what the Almighty can do
If with His love He befriend thee.

Praise to the Lord, oh, let all that is in me adore Him!
All that hath life and breath, come now with praises before Him.
Let the amen sound from His people again;
Gladly for aye we adore Him.[1]

Reflection and Realignment

What overwhelming assignment or task lies before you? What problem has gotten you weary and worn down? Apply one of God's promises from today's devotional reading to your specific challenge, and write out a prayer asking God for help.

DAY 2

I AM YOUR SHEPHERD

The needs around you are great, and you long to be up and about, tending to your responsibilities. But the needs within you are greater still. Cherish this time of enforced inactivity. I am your *Yahweh Ra'ah*, the Lord your shepherd. I will lead you beside still waters and restore your soul. I desire to give you a fresh revelation of Me as I impress My truth upon the depths of your heart. Will you listen to My voice?

Many are the voices that seek your attention. They battle for your time and steal your energy. Learn to hear My voice above the noise, for "in returning and rest you shall be saved; in quietness and confidence shall be your strength." I love you, My precious child, and always will. As one of My sheep, you will not be found wanting. I am the source of all your needs, and I will satisfy you completely. Settle your heart on the hope that is found in Me.

The entrance of My words gives light; it gives understanding to the simple. Meditate on My Word, and cherish it as your light. It will guide you through the dark, troubling paths of this life and enable you to see clearly so you will not lose your footing. As the light of My Word illuminates your way, you will grow in wisdom. Learn now to hear My voice above all others and let go of those things that clutter your thinking. This is your pathway to peace.

Psalm 23:1–3; Isaiah 30:15; Jeremiah 31:3; Psalm 119:130

God's Promises

The LORD is my shepherd; I shall not want. He makes me to lie down in green pastures; He leads me beside the still waters. He restores my soul; He leads me in the paths of righteousness for His name's sake. (Ps. 23:1–3)

Thus says the Lord GOD, the Holy One of Israel: "In returning and rest you shall be saved; in quietness and confidence shall be your strength." (Isa. 30:15)

My sheep hear My voice, and I know them, and they follow Me. And I give them eternal life, and they shall never perish; neither shall anyone snatch them out of My hand. (John 10:27–28)

My Prayer

Heavenly Father, thank You for being my gentle, loving shepherd and for caring for me. Be my guide through this time of uncertainty, and help me hear Your voice above all others. There is truly none like You, and only in You can I fully put my trust. Lord, thank You that You do not forsake those who seek You, that You are good to all, and that Your tender mercies are over all You have created. Even when the darkness consumes me, You are there. Help me stay on Your path and not be led away to another, for Your path brings peace, and in Your presence is fullness of joy. I surrender everything to You, oh God, and let go of those thoughts that clutter my thinking and distract me from Your presence. You know what is best for me, and I can trust You with my future. Lead me now by Your loving hand, and help me rest in the soft space of Your grace. In Jesus' name I pray. Amen.

Psalm 9:10; Psalm 145:9; Psalm 16:11

My Worship

He leadeth me! O blessed thought!
O words with heavenly comfort fraught!
Whate'er I do, where'er I be,
still 'tis God's hand that leadeth me.

He leadeth me, He leadeth me,
By His own hand He leadeth me;
His faithful foll'wer I would be,
For by His hand He leadeth me.

Sometimes 'mid scenes of deepest gloom,
Sometimes where Eden's bowers bloom,
By waters still, o'er troubled sea,
Still 'tis my God that leadeth me.

Lord, I would place my hand in Thine,
Nor ever murmur nor repine;
Content, whatever lot I see,
Since 'tis my God that leadeth me.

And when my task on earth is done,
When by Thy grace the vict'ry's won,
E'en death's cold wave I will not flee,
Since God through Jordan leadeth me.[2]

REFLECTION AND REALIGNMENT

Reflect on one way God has led you in the past. Write this experience down and then pray a prayer of gratitude, thanking God for His guidance in the past and His promise to guide you today.

DAY 3

I AM
God Most High

Many are your cares and concerns about the future. You wonder if you will ever get better and, if you don't, how you will cope with chronic illness. You worry that you might never again enjoy the joy of a walk in the fresh outdoors. Lay your fears down. Cease striving, and know that I am *El Elyon*, God Most High, who will perform all things for you. As God over all, I see the end from the beginning, and I have your future in My hands.

"My grace is sufficient for you" and more than enough to help you through this day, but it only comes one moment at a time. I am with you always, for "I will never leave you nor forsake you." I am in your present moment. Embrace this challenging time as a gift. Do not dwell on the past or hurriedly rush into the future. I am doing a new thing in you right now—a new beginning is about to burst forth. This process, however, will take time, and I need your wholehearted attention. I am preparing you for what is to come. Stay in this present moment and seek Me. Soak in My presence, and be filled.

I know your weaknesses, and I will allocate My power to fill your areas of need. My plans for you are perfect. Stop trying to figure out those plans. Let Me be God, and you be you. I have a mission for you that only you can fulfill. I have a purpose for you that only you can complete. Though you feel as if you are encountering a setback, I will use this time to propel you forward. I am strengthening your character through the tests you are facing. Trust Me. "My thoughts are not your thoughts, nor are your ways My ways." You may not understand all you see, but know that My ways are always best.

Psalm 91:1; Psalm 57:2; 2 Corinthians 12:9; Hebrews 13:5; Psalm 18:30; Exodus 9:16; James 1:1–3; Proverbs 3:5; Isaiah 55:8

God's Promises

You, whose name alone is the LORD, are the Most High over all the earth. (Ps. 83:18)

They remembered that God was their rock, and the Most High God their Redeemer. (Ps. 78:35)

I will cry out to God Most High, to God who performs all things for me. (Ps. 57:2)

He who dwells in the secret place of the Most High shall abide under the shadow of the Almighty. (Ps. 91:1)

My Prayer

Heavenly Father, God Most High, I praise You. Nothing is too difficult for You—including the details of my future. You know my struggles and my setbacks, and You will use all things for my good and Your glory. Thank You for always being with me. I know that I can trust You through this difficult time and that Your purposes for me will prevail. I set my eyes on You, Lord God. Help me live by faith and not by sight. In Jesus' name I pray. Amen.

Psalm 144:1; Job 19:25; Jeremiah 23:27; Romans 8:28; Isaiah 41:10; Job 42:2

My Worship

I sing the mighty pow'r of God
That made the mountains rise,
That spread the flowing seas abroad
And built the lofty skies.
I sing the wisdom that ordained
The sun to rule the day;
The moon shines full at His command,
And all the stars obey.

I sing the goodness of the Lord,
Who filled the earth with food;
He formed the creatures with His Word
And then pronounced them good.
Lord, how Thy wonders are displayed
Where'er I turn my eye,
If I survey the ground I tread
Or gaze upon the sky!

There's not a plant or flower below
But makes Thy glories known;

And clouds arise, and tempests blow
By order from thy throne;
While all that borrows life from Thee
Is ever in Thy care;
And everywhere that we can be
Thou, God, art present there.[3]

REFLECTION AND REALIGNMENT

What are your concerns about the future? Choose one of God's promises from today's devotional reading to claim over each care. Write these words: "Today I cast _____ upon the Lord and claim His promise over these concerns. I will trust Him with all the details of my future and not try to figure things out."

DAY 4

I AM
The Everlasting God

You are fretting about this time of dormancy in your life. But your worry about your family and their needs is not helpful. Quiet yourself in My presence, and know that I am *El Olam*, the eternal, everlasting God. I have no beginning and no end. I have always been and always will be. Because of this you can have the peaceful assurance that I am always with you, fully available to help you through the various seasons of your journey.

I neither faint nor grow weary, and My understanding is unsearchable. As your Creator, I formed you. As your eternal God, I follow you. As the first and the last, I love you, and My love for you will never end. Like a mother bird cares for her young and not one falls from her sight, so I care for you. My eyes scan the whole earth to strongly support My own.

Trust Me, My child, through the darkness, and trust Me through the light. I am sovereign over all your cares. Nothing is too hard for Me. See, I formed you, know all about you, and with My breath gave you life. Do I not also have the power to resolve the dilemmas you face? Surely I do. Instead of fretting, find rest. "Be still, and know that I am God." Though the road before you is full of potholes and deep valleys of difficulty, I am also there.

I go before you and make your crooked places straight. I also hem you in. Before you and behind you, I am there. Learn to embrace the low points in your journey as well as anticipate the high ones. Rest in Me, for I am your refuge, and underneath you are My everlasting arms.

Genesis 21:33; Isaiah 40:28; Psalm 139:13; Psalm 139:7–8; Jeremiah 31:3; 1 Corinthians 13:8; 2 Chronicles 16:9; Jeremiah 32:17; Job 33:4; Psalm 46:10; Isaiah 45:2; Psalm 139:5; Deuteronomy 33:27

God's Promises

Have you not known? Have you not heard? The everlasting God, the Lord, the Creator of the ends of the earth, neither faints nor is weary. His understanding is unsearchable. (Isa. 40:28)

Lord, You have been our dwelling place in all generations. Before the mountains were brought forth, or ever You had formed the earth and the world, even from everlasting to everlasting, You are God. (Ps. 90:1–2)

Have you not known? Have you not heard? The everlasting God, the Lord, the Creator of the ends of the earth, neither faints nor is weary. His understanding is unsearchable. He gives power to the weak, and to those who have no might He increases strength. (Isa. 40:28–29)

The eternal God is your refuge, and underneath are the everlasting arms. (Deut. 33:27)

I Am the Everlasting God

My Prayer

Heavenly Father, everlasting God, thank You that You are always with me. You are my refuge, a place where I can find shelter in times of trouble. You are my fortress, my place of security and protection. You are my God, in whom I trust. Please help me, in my moments of distress, to experience Your peace as I seek to embrace my journey. Although I don't like the low points, it is during these times that I learn the most. Thank You that I don't need to fear or fret but can have courage and confidence as I face the unknowns before me, for You are my strength and my stability, my stronghold and my sustainer. No matter what I go through, You are always there, and You are mighty. Thank You for being eternally faithful, intimately interested, and personally involved in every detail of my life. With You by my side, I am secure. In Jesus' name I pray. Amen.

Psalm 46:1; Psalm 18:2; Psalm 91:2; Psalm 43:2; Deuteronomy 32:4; Psalm 18:2; Psalm 54:4; Zephaniah 3:17

My Worship

Be still, my soul; the Lord is on thy side.
Bear patiently the cross of grief or pain.
Leave to thy God to order and provide;
In every change, He faithful will remain.
Be still, my soul; thy best, thy heav'nly Friend
Through thorny ways leads to a joyful end.

Be still, my soul; thy God doth undertake.
To guide the future as He has the past.

Thy hope, thy confidence, let nothing shake;
All now mysterious shall be bright at last.
Be still, my soul; the waves and winds still know.
His voice who ruled them while He dwelt below.

Be still, my soul; the hour is hast'ning on.
When we shall be forever with the Lord,
When disappointment, grief, and fear are gone,
Sorrow forgot, love's purest joys restored.
Be still, my soul; when change and tears are past,
All safe and blessed we shall meet at last.[4]

Reflection and Realignment

What is creating restlessness within your soul? Ask the Lord to help you identify it. Commit your cares to God in prayer, inviting His presence to guide you, and release those things that are causing you to feel unsettled.

DAY 5

I AM YOUR PEACE

You are worried and fearful about the unknowns in your future. Anxieties swell up inside your soul as you wonder what will happen to you and your family if you don't get better. But I am your peace, your *Yahweh Shalom*. Do not let fear consume you. There is nothing the enemy would like more than to incapacitate you with fear.

You forget that I am already in your future. You, however, must learn to live in the present—to embrace each moment as it comes. My peace is present with you in this moment. But when you try to figure out what is ahead, your thoughts move into the future, and you stop depending on Me. This is why fear and anxiety overtake you.

Hold on to My promises, for only they stand strong through the passage of time. They do not shift, waver, or move with the tides of life's volatile ordeals. Claim My promises over your future, and rest in them today. For I Myself have said, "I will never leave you nor forsake you." So you may boldly say, "The Lord is my helper; I will not fear. What can man do to me?" When your mind wanders anxiously ahead and you begin to fear what the future holds, stop your thoughts, and focus on Me. Do not fear the future. Focus on My presence that is with you today.

When I appeared to Gideon, I revealed Myself to him as his peace. Gideon then built an altar and called it "The-Lord-Is-Peace" in order to worship Me and provide a spiritual marker of his encounter with Me. What I said to Gideon I also say to you: "Peace be with you; do not fear." As your peace, your *Yahweh Shalom*, I will quiet you with My love and still your soul with My presence. I will shelter you in the protection of My wings and supply you with strength. I am the lifter of your countenance and the lover of your soul.

Rest now, My child, in My peaceful presence. Do not anxiously look ahead or fearfully look behind. Keep your eyes on Me. "Ponder the path of your feet, and let all your ways be established." In everything pray. Surrender all your cares and concerns to Me, and I will carry them. Anxiety and peace cannot flow from the same stream, and neither can fear and faith. Make the conscious choice today to allow faith to guide you and peace to rule in your heart. My plans for you are perfect.

Judges 6:23–24; Hebrews 13:5–6; Zephaniah 3:17; Psalm 62:5; Psalm 91:4; Psalm 29:11; Numbers 6:26; John 3:16; Proverbs 4:26; Philippians 4:6; Psalm 18:30

God's Promises

Peace I leave with you, My peace I give to you; not as the world gives do I give to you. Let not your heart be troubled, neither let it be afraid. (John 14:27)

You will keep him in perfect peace, whose mind is stayed on You, because he trusts in You. (Isa. 26:3)

Be strong and of good courage, do not fear nor be afraid of them; for the L ORD your God, He is the One who goes with you. He will not leave you nor forsake you. (Deut. 31:6)

My Prayer

Heavenly Father, thank You for Your peace. Though my circumstances seem all but peaceful right now, I can cling to You and find the refuge my soul so desperately needs. Thank You for meeting me in my difficulties and promising to guide me through my troubles. I am Yours, God of peace, and I will allow Your perfect peace to reign in my heart and flow through my life. Whenever I am afraid, I will trust in You. When I am unsure and doubts divide my soul, I will rest in Your presence, knowing that You are with me and that my future is secure in Your hands. In Jesus' name I pray. Amen.

Deuteronomy 31:6; Isaiah 43:2; Psalm 56:3; Jeremiah 29:11

My Worship

Be not dismayed whate'er betide,
God will take care of you;
Beneath His wings of love abide,
God will take care of you.

God will take care of you
Through every day, o'er all the way;

He will take care of you;
God will take care of you.

Through days of toil when heart doth fail,
God will take care of you;
When dangers fierce your path assail,
God will take care of you.

All you may need He will provide,
God will take care of you;
Nothing you ask will be denied,
God will take care of you.

No matter what may be the test,
God will take care of you;
Lean, weary one, upon His breast,
God will take care of you.[5]

Reflection and Realignment

Take a moment to reflect on your life, and consider a time when you encountered God as your peace, as Gideon did. Write John 14:27 on a piece of paper, and post it where you can see it often: "Peace I leave with you, My peace I give to you; not as the world gives do I give to you. Let not your heart be troubled, neither let it be afraid."

DAY 6

I AM
THE ONE WHO SEES

I see your broken heart and know your pain. Those closest to you do not understand your ongoing affliction, and you feel misunderstood and rejected by them. But I have not rejected you. You do not bear the weight of your distress alone, for I am *El Ro'i*, the God who sees and responds to your every need.

When Hagar fled from Sarai, I was with her. The harsh treatment she received did not go unnoticed. I saw her in her helpless state as she fled into the wilderness from her mistress, Sarai. In her despair I revealed Myself to her as My tender mercy met her in her time of deepest need. Abandoned, abused, ridiculed, and rejected, My love became her sanctuary, and My presence became her peace. In the same way, I am with you.

I collect your tears in a bottle; each one is precious. Though you cannot understand it now, your salty tears will one day be sweet as I reclaim for you that which has been stolen from you. Trust Me, My child—I make all things new. I do not allow anything to come into your life without giving it permission to do so, and I will use each and every incident for your good. Nothing is ever wasted in My hands. However, you must trust Me, have faith, and believe that I have a purpose for your pain and can produce something beautiful out of it in time.

My presence is with you. I am for you and not against you. Open your eyes to My love, and receive it as your gift. It is like a large comforting blanket; wear it, and allow it to warm your soul. It was made just for you to ease your pain through this time of sadness. Through My mercies you are not consumed, because My compassions do not fail. They are new every morning; great is My faithfulness.

I always see you, even in the darkest hour of your hurt and sorrow, and I am with you. I care for the birds of the air, and I extend My watch care over you as well. No matter how deep your pit, My love is deeper still, and no matter how high the mountain you must ascend, My love is higher. Rest in My love, dear one, and allow it to flood your soul, refreshing your aching heart and restoring your joy. Drink deeply of My living water as we travel through this desert time together, and you will receive all the strength you need to continue the upward climb. From the top of the highest mountain to the depths of the deepest sea, My right hand will hold you, and My presence will be your guide.

Psalm 34:18; Isaiah 53:4; Genesis 16:6–13; Psalm 56:8;
Revelation 21:5; Romans 8:28, 31; Lamentations 3:22–23;
Matthew 6:26; Psalm 139:10

God's Promises

The eyes of the LORD are in every place, keeping watch on the evil and the good. (Prov. 15:3)

The righteous cry out, and the LORD hears, and delivers them out of all their troubles. The LORD is near to those who have a broken heart, and saves such as have a contrite spirit. (Ps. 34:17–18)

The eyes of the LORD run to and fro throughout the whole earth, to show Himself strong on behalf of those whose heart is loyal to Him. (2 Chron. 16:9)

My Prayer

Father God, thank You that You see me and know my needs, and thank You that Your Word promises that You shall supply all my needs according to Your riches in glory. No detail in my life escapes Your view. Oh, how I need You now in my time of trouble and ask that You would lift my heavy heart with Your love. Open my eyes to believe again, to grasp Your promises as my own even when my burdens seem impossible to bear. Many are my hurts, but You see every one. You are aware of all I am going through and will never leave me or abandon me to figure a way out of my troubles on my own. You want me to trust You, depend on You, walk through my difficulties with eyes of faith, knowing that You will either resolve my troubles or give me the grace and strength to get through them. Thank You for being with me, knowing me, and loving me unconditionally. Even when my heart is overwhelmed, I will trust in You and settle my soul on Your promises. In Jesus' name I pray. Amen.

Philippians 4:19; Deuteronomy 31:6

My Worship

Broken promises, they are so real;
Broken people, without any tears.
Broken dreams, they tear a heart in two;
Broken cisterns, empty of all that's true.

You are the living water; I come to You.
You heal the heart that's broken; You are true.
The true and living water, refresh me now;
Fill me to overflowing so I can be poured out.

Broken children with their silent cries;
No one hears them, but their pain can't be denied.
Searching for something to fill the void;
Empty cisterns, with nothing to provide.[6]

Reflection and Realignment

Ponder the truth that God sees you in your moments of pain. Now write down the areas of your life that are causing you heartache, and for each area write next to it "covered by God's love." God has you covered—even your heartaches and heartbreaks. Resolve today to allow His love to be your sanctuary and His presence to be your peace. He is near. He sees every broken heart and will love you through your time of sorrow.

DAY 7

I AM
Your Sanctifier

You are carrying the weight of shame like a noose around your neck. Painful childhood memories have held you prisoner for many years, and now, in this time of quiet reflection, they rear their ugly heads. Over the years you have allowed shame to disqualify you from accepting the value I have placed upon you. But I am your *Yahweh Mekaddishchem*, the Lord who sanctifies you. When I see you, I see My Son, who is pure, holy, and blameless.

I love you. As a fresh-flowing stream nourishes the parched ground around it, so My love flows into the deepest recesses of your soul to heal the hurts that cut so deep. Resolve today to remove the noose of shame and put on the royal robe of My love. Display it proudly, for you are My child. No matter how others see you or how you view yourself, I see you as flawless, full of infinite worth. Even before you were born, I knew you, crowned you with compassion, and received you as My very own. In My love for you, I constantly rejoice over you on both your good days and your bad ones.

Receive My love, and allow it to quiet your storm-tossed soul. Accept My love, and allow it to set you free. Past memories haunt you; they push you into a pit of despair. Bring these memories to Me. Lay them at My feet, and receive the healing, wholeness, and restoration that My love provides. My Son, Jesus Christ, bore your sin and shame on the cross. Through His sacrifice I have reclaimed and renamed you as My own. You are Mine.

Receive the free gift of My Son's sacrifice for you, and allow it to propel you forward to live an abundant, unhindered life. I have set you apart for a special purpose that only you can fulfill. Embrace your inheritance, and shine!

Exodus 31:13; Leviticus 20:7–8; 2 Corinthians 5:21;
Psalm 139:13–16; Zephaniah 3:17; 1 Peter 2:24; Romans 8:16–17;
1 John 3:1; John 10:10; Psalm 4:3

God's Promises

May the God of peace Himself sanctify you completely; and may your whole spirit, soul, and body be preserved blameless at the coming of our Lord Jesus Christ. He who calls you is faithful, who also will do it. (1 Thess. 5:23–24)

Do not fear, for you will not be ashamed; neither be disgraced, for you will not be put to shame; for you will forget the shame of your youth. (Isa. 54:4)

Instead of your shame you shall have double honor, and instead of confusion they shall rejoice in their portion. (Isa. 61:7)

I will greatly rejoice in the LORD, my soul shall be joyful in my God; for He has clothed me with the garments of salvation, He has covered me with the robe of righteousness, as a bridegroom decks himself with ornaments, and as a bride adorns herself with her jewels. (Isa. 61:10)

My Prayer

Heavenly Father, thank You for sanctifying me. I am no longer the person I used to be. Through Your free gift of sanctification through Your Son's death on the cross, I have been made new, set apart for what You have for me to do. Thank You for sending Your Son. I am no longer condemned, because He and I are one. Free from my burden of sin, shame, and guilt, I can now live unhindered by the blood of Jesus that was spilled. Because of Christ's sacrifice, I am healed. I am free. Thank You, Lord, my sanctifier, for sanctifying me. In Jesus' name I pray. Amen.

Ephesians 2:10; John 3:16; Romans 8:1; 1 Peter 2:24

My Worship

Be Thou my vision, O Lord of my heart;
Naught be all else to me, save that Thou art;
Thou my best thought, by day or by night,
Waking or sleeping, Thy presence my light.

Be Thou my wisdom, and Thou my true word;
I ever with Thee and Thou with me, Lord;
Thou my great Father, I Thy true son;
Thou in me dwelling, and I with Thee one.

Riches I heed not, nor man's empty praise,
Thou mine inheritance, now and always;
Thou and Thou only, first in my heart,
High King of heaven, my treasure Thou art.

High King of heaven, my victory won,
May I reach heaven's joys, O bright heav'n's Sun!
Heart of my own heart, whate'er befall,
Still be my vision, O ruler of all.[7]

Reflection and Realignment

God's Word is clear that "instead of your shame you will have double honor" (Isa. 61:7). Allow this promise to sink deep into your soul. Meditate on it, and release any shame that has hindered your progress as God's beloved child. You are set free! Seek to become the person God wants you to be!

DAY 8

I AM
Your Healer

Do not allow complaining and resentment to withhold My favor from you. Soul wounds of many years' making have created deep, unmet longings within you that tempt you to be bitter. Precious child, I am your *Yahweh Rapha*, the Lord your healer. I desire to quench your thirst—to spiritually revive the dryness in your soul and heal you of any bitterness and pain.

When the Israelites walked from the Red Sea through the wilderness of Shur, they found no water. For three days they were thirsty, parched, and dry like the desert ground around them. They desperately sought a thirst quencher, but nothing was found—only the bitter waters of Marah. Complaining and grumbling, they went to Moses, saying, "What shall we drink?" Moses had no answer, but he sought My presence, and I showed him a tree. Casting the tree into the bitter waters, the waters were made sweet and quenched the people's thirst.

As your *Yahweh Rapha*, I will provide you with living water—water that fully satisfies, that will quench the longings of your unfulfilled heart and restore the strength that overwhelming trials have stolen from you. That living water is My love. My love is also the salve that will heal your wounded soul and soothe your aching heart.

Open your eyes to see My love, and open your hands to receive it. I realize that you are apprehensive. Your hurts keep you at a distance from Me. Your guard is up, and your mind is cynical. That is understandable, but this is not My way for you. Do not be restless. I want you to relax. My presence goes with you, and I will give you rest. Diligently heed My voice, and praise Me even through your pain. When you do, you'll experience My love—the greatest of all gifts.

I desire to lavish My love upon you and prosper you in all things. But you must first learn to embrace My abundant love and allow it to embrace you abundantly. Do not compare Me to others who have disappointed you by placing conditions on their love for you. Human love can be volatile, dependent on feelings. My love for you is unconditional, has no limits, cannot be measured, and endures forever. My love "bears all things, believes all things, hopes all things, endures all things. My love never fails." Before you were born, I chose you. I know all about you and love you just the same. There is nothing you can do, think, or say that will ever change My love for you. My love is everlasting.

Like the constant ripple in a flowing stream, so My love constantly washes over you. The fresh waters of My love are present to heal your sun-parched soul as you travel through this weary land. The waters of My love run deeper than you could ever imagine and for longer than you could ever comprehend. My love for you is perfect. It can never be changed, removed, minimized, or depleted—but it can be ignored. The choice is up to you: will you receive My love today? It is a gift, freely given to those who seek it and abundantly given to satisfy your deepest longings.

Exodus 15:22–26; Exodus 33:14; 1 Corinthians 13:13;
Psalm 1:3; Psalm 136:26; 1 Corinthians 13:7–8; Ephesians 1:4–5;
1 John 3:1; Jeremiah 31:3

God's Promises

O Lord my God, I cried out to You, and You healed me. (Ps. 30:2)

They cried out to the Lord in their trouble, and He saved them out of their distresses. He sent His word and healed them, and delivered them from their destructions. (Ps. 107:19–20)

He heals the brokenhearted and binds up their wounds. (Ps. 147:3)

Whoever drinks of the water that I shall give him will never thirst. But the water that I shall give him will become in him a fountain of water springing up into everlasting life. (John 4:14)

My Prayer

Father God, thank You for healing my pain-filled soul with Your powerful love. I acknowledge that sometimes I lose sight of Your love and overlook the healing it provides. Forgive me for taking my eyes off You and looking to other sources for love. Only You can love me like no other, and only Your love can fully satisfy. I choose now to receive Your boundless, pure, perfect love, and I invite You to apply Your healing salve to those areas of my heart and soul that need to be set free. In accordance with Your Word, I resist the devil, and I submit to You, oh God. I acknowledge that only Your love, Lord, can heal my hurts that cut so deeply. I draw near to You and receive Your love, believing that its presence and power will perfect me. In Jesus' name I pray. Amen.

James 4:7; Isaiah 53:5

My Worship

The love of God is greater far
Than tongue or pen can ever tell;
It goes beyond the highest star,
And reaches to the lowest hell;
The guilty pair, bowed down with care,
God gave His Son to win;
His erring child He reconciled,
And pardoned from his sin.

Oh, love of God, how rich and pure!
How measureless and strong!
It shall forevermore endure—
The saints' and angels' song.

When years of time shall pass away,
And earthly thrones and kingdoms fall,
When men, who here refuse to pray,
On rocks and hills and mountains call,
God's love so sure, shall still endure,
All measureless and strong;
Redeeming grace to Adam's race—
The saints' and angels' song.

> Could we with ink the ocean fill,
> And were the skies of parchment made,
> Were every stalk on earth a quill,
> And every man a scribe by trade,
> To write the love of God above,
> Would drain the ocean dry.
> Nor could the scroll contain the whole,
> Though stretched from sky to sky.[8]

Reflection and Realignment

What do you need to be healed from? Write out a prayer asking your *Yahweh Rapha* to touch this area of your life with His healing power. Now with open hands receive the outcome to your petition, and trust God to fulfill His healing work in your life in His perfect timing and way.

DAY 9

I AM
Your All-Sufficient One

Your heart aches from the wrongs done against you. Your emotions vacillate between anger and sadness toward those you feel should understand and walk with you through your tough times but don't. You lack the ability to forgive them, but I am your *El Shaddai*, God Almighty, your all-sufficient One, and I will provide all you lack and bless you exceedingly. In the same way I established My covenant with Abraham, so I have established My promises with you. These promises are found in My Word, the Bible. Meditate on My promises instead of your own thoughts and feelings, and receive My words as your soul sustenance.

Your heart is breaking, and you feel that no one sees your pain. But I see your pain. I not only see it, but I am experiencing it with you. You are not alone. I go before you, and I am with you. I will never abandon you or leave your side.

Allow My love to sweep over you and sustain you through this time. Many are your sufferings in this world. Disappointments will come your way, sorrow will grieve your soul, and unmet expectations will burrow their way into your heart. But how you respond to your sufferings will determine whether the hurt will make you bitter or better. Through My tender mercy I will shine light into your darkness and guide your feet in the way of peace.

It is never too late for a new beginning. Your former habit of being weighed down is not My way for you. I want you to walk in newness of life and receive the gifts I give. That which has been stolen from you I will give back to you and even more. "I will restore to you the years that the swarming locust has eaten, the crawling locust, the consuming locust, and the chewing locust." As your sufficiency, I am the source of all your blessings. Nothing is impossible for Me. I will sustain you and satisfy you completely.

I offer you My grace freely, and it is sufficient to soothe your aching heart. But in receiving My grace, you must also forgive the wrongs done against you, just as My Son did as He hung on the cross. If you dwell upon the wrongdoing of others, it will poison your soul.

Determine today to live in My peace. Choose forgiveness over resentment, and replace any bitterness with My love. This is a hard task, but it is possible as you set your sights on Me. Choosing My love is the door to your freedom, and loving your enemies is the key that unlocks that door.

Genesis 17:1–2; Deuteronomy 31:8; John 16:33; Luke 1:78–79; Joel 2:25; Luke 1:37; Romans 3:24; Romans 12:18; Ephesians 4:32

God's Promises

God is able to make all grace abound toward you, that you, always having all sufficiency in all things, may have an abundance for every good work. (2 Cor. 9:8)

Not that we are sufficient of ourselves to think of anything as being from ourselves, but our sufficiency is from God. (2 Cor. 3:5)

I Am Your All-Sufficient One

Whenever you stand praying, if you have anything against anyone, forgive him, that your Father in heaven may also forgive you your trespasses. (Mark 11:25)

He said to me, "My grace is sufficient for you, for My strength is made perfect in weakness." Therefore most gladly I will rather boast in my infirmities, that the power of Christ may rest upon me. (2 Cor. 12:9)

My Prayer

Heavenly Father, God Almighty, all-sufficient One, only You can supply my lack and enable me to forgive. You are the source of all my blessings and the sustainer of my life. Even in the midst of the most difficult situations, You are there. Nothing is hidden from Your view, and according to Your Word, nothing is impossible for You. Resolve the frustrations within my heart and help me forgive. I cannot do this on my own. My memories are so powerful, and my hurt is so deep. Come into my life and give me a new heart—a heart that is full of Your love, Your joy, and Your peace. Fill my emptiness with Your abundance, and lavish Your strength upon me where I am weak. I exchange my thoughts for Your thoughts and my ways for Your ways. Help me be different, oh God. I don't want to be ruled by my flesh; I want to be ruled by Your Spirit. Help me walk in obedience to Your Word and have compassion toward those who have wronged me. In Jesus' name I pray. Amen.

Hebrews 4:13; Luke 1:37

My Worship

Lord, today I give You me.
I am nothing without Thee.
Lord, take my life, and let it be
An offering, all to Thee.

You are my all in all;
You are my King;
You are my Prince of Peace;
You comfort me.

Lord, today I celebrate
Your mighty power, and I consecrate
My life to You, the great I AM;
I give to You all that I am.

Lord, today I stand in awe;
Your awesome presence makes me fall
Down on my knees; my humble plea,
Take my life, and let it be.[9]

Reflection and Realignment

The name *El Shaddai* means "all-sufficient One." In what area of your life do you feel that you are lacking? Commit to praying daily over this matter, asking God, your *El Shaddai*, to be your sufficiency. He promises to give you His grace to see you through your troubling time.

DAY 10

I AM
Your Banner

My child, your shattered dreams are not in vain. They are actually a piece of a puzzle. You thrived on being strong and capable to care for your family and help others, but the loss of these things doesn't mean your life is over. I will use the pain of your broken dreams to create something beautiful, for I am your *Yahweh Nissi*, the Lord your banner. As your banner, I go before you into battle—the battle to believe Me for a hopeful future.

I bring hope to your heart and empower you with My strength. Your outlook may seem grim, but victory is in My hand: "Do not let your heart faint, do not be afraid, and do not tremble or be terrified because of them; for the LORD your God is He who goes with you, to fight for you against your enemies, to save you."

You cannot understand or even see the end result of this season right now; all you can do is grieve. But that is okay. I have created you to be cleansed by your tears. Do not hold them back; let them roll freely, and as they do, allow My love to wash over you. Your tears are the testimony of a great work I am doing, and with My help you will be able to dream once again.

For now, My child, rest in My love. Allow it to embrace you and soothe your aching heart. Even the most difficult things in life can become a source of strength and wisdom for the journey that lies ahead. Allow the passage of time to help you make peace with your current reality. There is no need to rush the process.

The battle is great, but I am greater! Just as I gave victory to Joshua and the Israelites over the Amalekites, so will I give victory to you. Your foe—that disappointment that drags you down—is not beyond My limitless reach. I have the power to eradicate any opposition that comes against you with a wave of My almighty hand. But you must look to Me, your foe fighter, as Moses did as he sat on the hilltop above the battle. He did not lift a sword but rather his hands in prayer. As Joshua and his men battled in the valley, Moses sought Me continually. Whenever his arms were lifted toward heaven, Israel prevailed in battle. Whenever he lowered his arms, Israel began to lose. Seeing that his arms were heavy and ready to drop, Aaron and Hur came alongside to provide him support, keeping his hands steady until sunset when victory was won. You too, My child, can have victory over any foe as you keep your hands lifted up toward Me.

I am your banner, and I go before you. No battle is too great and no foe too fierce for Me. Seek My face, precious child, in the midst of your battle to hope. Wait upon Me, and I will see you through. Receive My love, and allow it to penetrate the depths of your heart, nourishing a new dream beneath the ashes. A new season is coming. A new day is dawning. I will make a road in your wilderness and a river in your desert. Trust Me, My child. Your victory is sure. "Peace I leave with you, My peace I give to you; not as the world gives do I give to you. Let not your heart be troubled, neither let it be afraid."

Exodus 17:8–15; Deuteronomy 20:3–4; Isaiah 43:19; John 14:27

God's Promises

Moses built an altar and called its name, The-Lord-Is-My-Banner. (Exod. 17:15)

Hear, O Israel: Today you are on the verge of battle with your enemies. Do not let your heart faint, do not be afraid, and do not tremble or be terrified because of them; for the Lord your God is He who goes with you, to fight for you against your enemies, to save you. (Deut. 20:3–4)

Why are you cast down, O my soul? And why are you disquieted within me? Hope in God, for I shall yet praise Him for the help of His countenance. (Ps. 42:5)

I know the thoughts that I think toward you, says the Lord, thoughts of peace and not of evil, to give you a future and a hope. (Jer. 29:11)

My Prayer

Father God, thank You for being my banner. I call upon Your great name to protect me through this battle to hope in the face of broken dreams. As my banner, You will go before me and cover me with Your protective shield. I receive Your peace right now, and I ask You to restore hope to my heart through this time of adversity. This battle is not mine but Yours. Give me the wisdom and discernment to navigate the dark paths before me. According to Your Word, when I fall, I will arise; when I sit in darkness, You will be a light to me. Provide me the courage to stand strong in You and the ability to be fearless. Thank You for Your abiding presence. I am not alone, for You are with me. You are for me, not against me, and You are able to see me through. I stand in Your mighty power, and I invite Your presence to be my protection through this volatile time. In Jesus' name I pray. Amen.

Psalm 7:10; Micah 7:8

My Worship

O God, our help in ages past,
Our hope for years to come,
Our shelter from the stormy blast,
And our eternal home!

Under the shadow of Thy throne,
Still may we dwell secure;
Sufficient is Thine arm alone,
And our defense is sure.

Before the hills in order stood,
Or earth received her frame,
From everlasting, Thou art God,
To endless years the same.

A thousand ages in Thy sight,
Are like an ev'ning gone;
Short as the watch that ends the night,
Before the rising sun.

> Time, like an ever-rolling stream,
> Bears all its sons away;
> They fly forgotten, as a dream
> Dies at the opening day.
>
> O God, our help in ages past,
> Our hope for years to come;
> Be Thou our guide while life shall last,
> And our eternal home.[10]

Reflection and Realignment

What battle are you facing? Write down one of God's promises from today's devotional reading to claim over your struggle. With your hands lifted toward heaven, pray aloud, "Lord, I entrust my battle to You, and in faith I receive the victory that You are able to have over it. I will no longer allow this difficulty to consume me. I place my full trust and confidence in You, knowing that the outcome of this problem is in Your hands."

DAY 11

I AM
Your Provider

The tension in your heart is growing. This is not My way for you. You are trying to figure out the future and resolve the past. Memories haunt you, unmet expectations steal your joy, and disappointments weigh you down. But I am *Yahweh Yir'eh*, your provider. I can sufficiently meet all your needs. When Abraham needed a substitutionary sacrifice, I supplied for him, and I have supplied for you as well. Everything and anything that could possibly have inhibited you from living an abundant life was divinely taken away on Mount Calvary. Because of this, you are free—free to be all I created you to be!

The greatest disappointments you struggle with are those of your own doing. Mistakes you have made in the past have had far-reaching effects. If only you could rewind the film of your life, you would do things differently. Stop beating yourself up for the choices you have made. My grace covers your faults and failures. Give all your mistakes over to Me, and allow My grace to abound where you have fallen short. What's done is done; you cannot change the past. Use the past as a mentor to provide wisdom in the present and give guidance for the future.

When I asked Abraham to offer his son, Isaac, as a sacrifice on the mount of Moriah, at the very moment he raised the knife, I sent an angel to stop him and provided a ram for him to sacrifice. So I have provided for you. More than two thousand years ago, My one and only Son, Jesus Christ, took all your faults, failures, sin, shame, and guilt upon His body as He died on the cross. Stand in your freedom today, and stop allowing your past to define you. Choose this day to follow Me.

The best way to resolve the tension within your soul is to choose contentment. Contentment is not a gift freely given but a lesson learned as you allow My love to rule in your heart. Trust that My assignments are appropriate, My ways are perfect, and My thoughts toward you are good, and you will find peaceful contentment in the plans I have for you and the provisions I make. Trust Me, My child. Ultimately accepting what was, is, and is to come will break the tension that grips your soul and set you free to enjoy the gifts of peace and contentment that My love provides.

Genesis 22:13–14; Isaiah 53:5; Philippians 4:11

God's Promises

Abraham lifted his eyes and looked, and there behind him was a ram caught in a thicket by its horns. So Abraham went and took the ram, and offered it up for a burnt offering instead of his son. And Abraham called the name of the place, The-Lord-Will-Provide; as it is said to this day, "In the Mount of the Lord it shall be provided." (Gen. 22:13–14)

I Am Your Provider

My God shall supply all your need according to His riches in glory by Christ Jesus. (Phil. 4:19)

His divine power has given to us all things that pertain to life and godliness, through the knowledge of Him who called us by glory and virtue. (2 Pet. 1:2–3)

Come to Me, all you who labor and are heavy laden, and I will give you rest. Take My yoke upon you and learn from Me, for I am gentle and lowly in heart, and you will find rest for your souls. For My yoke is easy and My burden is light. (Matt. 11:28–30)

My Prayer

Father God, my provider, thank You for providing for me on Calvary so I can lay all my tensions down at the foot of the cross. I am extremely blessed, for Your divine power has given me all things pertaining to life and godliness. Though I cannot turn back the clock and change the way I did things in the past, I can live differently today. Thank You for giving me a new beginning and lavishing Your love upon me. I want to walk in Your love and in faith receive the plans that You have for me. I am just a weak vessel, but in You I am strong. Thank You, Lord, for not giving up on me. I will walk in Your delight and not in discouragement. I choose faith over fear. I am certain that You will sufficiently meet all my needs, and from this day forward I say to my soul, "I trust You, God." Thank You for giving me a new beginning with a new purpose to fulfill. In Jesus' name I pray. Amen.

2 Peter 1:3; Jeremiah 29:11; 2 Corinthians 12:10; Philippians 4:19

My Worship

Open my eyes, that I may see
Glimpses of truth Thou hast for me;
Place in my hands the wonderful key
That shall unclasp and set me free.

Silently now I wait for Thee,
Ready, my God, Thy will to see.
Open my eyes; illumine me, Spirit divine.

Open my ears, that I may hear
Voices of truth Thou sendest clear;
And while the wave notes fall on my ear,
Everything false will disappear.

Open my mouth, and let me bear
Gladly the warm truth everywhere;
Open my heart and let me prepare
Love with Thy children thus to share.

Open my mind, that I may read
More of Thy love in word and deed.
What shall I fear while yet Thou dost lead?
Only for light from Thee I plead.[11]

Reflection and Realignment

Think of those decisions from your past that you would make differently if given another chance. Now imagine that you are a part of the crowd standing before the cross at Jesus' crucifixion more than two thousand years ago. You are weighed down by your faults and failures as you carry them like a loaded sack on your back. You take off that sack, and you place it at the foot of the cross. Now write down the date and these words: "Today I receive the abundant life God has for me. I am no longer a prisoner to _____, for God's Word says in John 8:36, 'If the Son makes you free, you shall be free indeed.'"

DAY 12

I AM
Your Constant Companion

You have allowed many cares to distract you from My love. Your efforts to come up with solutions to your problems and concerns offer you an escape, and for a time they pacify your deep, unmet needs, but in the end they leave you feeling empty. Your longing for answers will never be completely satisfied in substitutes. Only My love can fully satisfy you and fill the holes in your heart. Come to Me, My child, and I will be your constant companion. I am *Yahweh Shammah*, the Lord your God who is there, and I will delight your heart.

Your healing will begin when you recognize that your attraction to eternal substitutes cannot be overcome by your own power. It is only through My power that you can flee the temptations that divert your attention from Me. I am your refuge and strength, your help in each moment, the One who is right there with you and able to see you through.

My presence is not contained in a tabernacle or a church building; My presence is with you wherever you go. When you need Me, I am there. Even when you do not feel that you need Me, I am still there. I am fully accessible at all times to all who seek Me with all their hearts. You are never alone. My presence fully resides within you through the Holy Spirit. Allow this truth to transform your thinking: "I am with you always."

Anything you seek more than Me is an idol. Therefore, My beloved child, flee from those idols. Divinely empowered by the authority given through the precious blood of My Son, break free from substitutes for My love, and return to Me. Only My love can heal the deepest wounds and completely satisfy your soul.

Ezekiel 48:35; Psalm 46:1; Joshua 1:9; Jeremiah 29:13; John 14:16;
Matthew 28:20; 1 Corinthians 10:14

God's Promises

Behold, the tabernacle of God is with men, and He will dwell with them, and they shall be His people. God Himself will be with them and be their God. And God will wipe away every tear from their eyes; there shall be no more death, nor sorrow, nor crying. There shall be no more pain, for the former things have passed away. (Rev. 21:3–4)

Do you not know that you are the temple of God and that the Spirit of God dwells in you? (1 Cor. 3:16)

Fear not, for I am with you; be not dismayed, for I am your God. I will strengthen you, yes, I will help you, I will uphold you with My righteous right hand. (Isa. 41:10)

Have I not commanded you? Be strong and of good courage; do not be afraid, nor be dismayed, for the Lord your God is with you wherever you go. (Josh. 1:9)

My Prayer

Heavenly Father, thank You for always being there and for being my constant companion. I have sought substitutes to fill the voids within my heart rather than wholeheartedly seeking You. Please forgive me, and help me find my full satisfaction in You. Fuel my passion for You, and help me experience more of You in my life. I know that You are near. You are always with me, and You are my forever friend. No one can snatch me out of Your hand, for You have promised to be my present help. Help me set my mind on things above, not on things of this earth, for all my life's troubles and disappointments are used as tools in Your hands. Nothing comes into my life unless You have given it permission to do so. Enable me to see my circumstances through Your eyes and fully trust You with all things. From this point until eternity, You are with me and will fully satisfy my heart. In Jesus' name I pray. Amen.

Matthew 28:20; John 10:29; Psalm 46:1–3;
Colossians 3:2

My Worship

Blessed golden ray,
Like a star of glory,
Lighting up my way!
Through the clouds of midnight,
This bright promise shone,
"I will never leave thee,
Never will leave thee alone."

No, never alone,
No, never alone;
He promised never to leave me,
Never to leave me alone;
No, never alone,
No, never alone;
He promised never to leave me,
Never to leave me alone.

Roses fade around me,
Lilies bloom and die,
Earthly sunbeams vanish—
Radiant still the sky!
Jesus, Henna-flower,
Blooming for His own,
Jesus, heaven's sunshine,
Never will leave me alone.

Steps unseen before me,
Hidden dangers near;
Nearer still my Savior,
Whispering, "Be of cheer";
Joys, like birds of springtime,
To my heart have flown,
Singing all so sweetly,
"He will not leave me alone."[12]

REFLECTION AND REALIGNMENT

Often idols can linger in our hearts without our awareness. Write out a prayer asking God to reveal any idols (comfort, control, career, pleasure, approval, success, fame, fortune, etc.) within your heart that draw your attention from God to yourself or other things. Repent of each idol God reveals to you, and invite God's presence to recapture your heart and reclaim it as His rightful throne.

DAY 13

I AM

Your Lord Almighty

Some time has passed since you have recognized My presence and power in your life. You have allowed the tensions of this world and the cares within your soul to consume you. But I am *Yahweh Tzeva'ot*, the Lord of hosts, the Lord Almighty. I am chief overall, and every power in heaven and on Earth is under My command. I know all. I see all. I am sovereign over all. Never can My rule be overshadowed or taken over, for I am the Lord Almighty, and there is none like Me. Call upon Me, and I will answer you and work powerfully in your situation.

My presence is with you, and it is a gift—so open it! It surrounds you and satisfies you; it revives you and strengthens you. If you lose sight of My presence, it will be your downfall. I love you too much to allow you to fall into a pit. Focus your eyes back on Me, My child, and learn to maintain a heavenly perspective through all your troubles.

The problems you are encountering have occupied your attention for too long and are creating tension within your soul. Like a dark storm cloud, these problems tend to overshadow the rays of My Son. But this is not My way for you. I want you to rest in My heavenly rays and allow them to revive you. I am with you always, and My thoughts of you are always good. Through the trials I am training you to recognize Me. Experiencing My presence when your faith is shaken is difficult for you to do, but it is possible. I will give you the ability. The pressures of this life will only continue to drive you down into despair until you choose to see Me in the midst of them all.

My provisions for you are limitless, and My defense of you is sure. When David confronted the giant Goliath, I was with him, and I will also be with you. As David armed himself with My presence and faced the giant with My power, his victory was won. Goliath was defeated, and My purposes prevailed.

As the Lord of hosts, nothing, absolutely nothing, can thwart My plans for you. I am the sovereign One, in control over all things. People may reject you, ridicule you, persecute you, and abandon you, but I never will. Stand strong, My child, in the strength and power of My might, for I, the Lord of hosts, the Lord God Almighty, am with you!

Psalm 46:7; Jeremiah 10:6–7; Jeremiah 33:3; Matthew 28:20;
Jeremiah 29:11; 2 Peter 1:3; Psalm 94:22; 1 Samuel 17:45–46;
2 Chronicles 20:6; Deuteronomy 31:8; Ephesians 6:10

God's Promises

O Lord God of hosts, who is mighty like You, O Lord? Your faithfulness also surrounds You. (Ps. 89:8)

Behold, He who forms mountains, and creates the wind, who declares to man what his thought is, and makes the morning darkness, who treads the high places of the earth—the Lord God of hosts is His name. (Amos 4:13)

The LORD of hosts is with us; the God of Jacob is our refuge. (Ps. 46:7)

Even the sparrow has found a home, and the swallow a nest for herself, where she may lay her young—even Your altars, O LORD of hosts, my King and my God. (Ps. 84:3)

He who dwells in the secret place of the Most High shall abide under the shadow of the Almighty. I will say of the LORD, "He is my refuge and my fortress; my God, in Him I will trust." (Ps. 91:1–2)

My Prayer

Father God, Lord of hosts, God Almighty, I come humbly before Your throne of grace to praise and exalt Your great name. No matter the difficulties that surround me, You alone are worthy of my worship. Forgive me for the many times I have taken my eyes off You and walked away to try to figure out or fix my dilemmas. I commit myself to You today; I need more of You in my life. Help me follow You and flow with Your Spirit instead of trying to forcefully make things more to my liking. Increase my faith, Lord, to see You in every detail of my life, and increase my awareness of Your almighty presence with me through this day. In Jesus' name I pray. Amen.

Zechariah 4:6; Hebrews 4:16; Luke 17:5

My Worship

A mighty fortress is our God,
A bulwark never failing;
Our helper He amid the flood
Of mortal ills prevailing.
For still our ancient foe
Doth seek to work us woe;
His craft and power are great
And armed with cruel hate;
On earth is not his equal.

Did we in our own strength confide,
Our striving would be losing;
Were not the right man on our side,
The Man of God's own choosing.
Dost ask who that may be?
Christ Jesus—it is He;
Lord Sabaoth, His name,
From age to age the same,
And He must win the battle.

And though this world, with devils filled,
Should threaten to undo us,
We will not fear, for God hath willed
His truth to triumph through us.
The prince of darkness grim—
We tremble not for him;
His rage we can endure,
For lo, his doom is sure;
One little word shall fell him.

That word above all earthly pow'rs,
No thanks to them, abideth;
The Spirit and the gifts are ours
Through Him who with us sideth.
Let goods and kindred go,
This mortal life also;
The body they may kill;
God's truth abideth still;
His kingdom is forever.[13]

Reflection and Realignment

What stressful situation in your life needs God's almighty intervention? Invite His powerful presence into your predicament. As you consider what you are struggling with, choose one of God's promises, either one from today's reading or another from His Word, to claim over it. Commit your need to the Lord, and in faith trust Him for the outcome.

DAY 14

I AM
Your Righteousness

My child, fear has a tight grip on your life. It consumes you and keeps you from venturing beyond your comfort zone. Exploring unknown and uncharted territory is difficult for you; you would much rather spend your time where you know it is safe. Though this is understandable, there is a better way. Trust Me, My child, for I am *Yahweh Tzidkenu*, the Lord your righteousness, the One who gives you a new heart and puts a new spirit within you. As you pray and seek My face, I will show you how to navigate all the unknowns before you.

This is part of your faith walk—fully trusting Me when you cannot see what lies ahead. Remember, "faith is the substance of things hoped for, the evidence of things not seen." So when you come upon a crossroads between the path of fear and the path of faith, which will you take? Peace is inevitable when you follow the path I have for you. Unlike the path of fear, which can lead you to seek security in someone or something other than Me, the path of faith contains many unknowns that can be navigated only by fully trusting Me. Today you have a choice: will you choose fear or faith?

I will not only lead you to paths of righteousness, but I will also *be* your righteousness. Though you fall short of My perfection,

I still love you, and through that love I will freely and fully restore you. As I restore you to right relationship with Me, I will also restore you to right relationship with others. But this will take time. And it cannot come about by your own efforts—no matter how hard you try, you can attain righteousness only through faith in the finished work of My Son, Jesus Christ. I made Him who knew no sin to be made sin for you so that you might be made righteous in My sight.

My dearly beloved child, you know the right path to take, but the battle to trust wages in your mind. Stop trying to figure things out. Resolve today to choose faith and allow My Spirit to guide you. Glorious vistas are waiting to be seen as you scale this mountainous path. Today commit to allowing faith to rule in your heart, and when fear comes knocking, stand firm and keep trusting Me with every fiber of your being.

Jeremiah 23:5–6; Ezekiel 36:26; Hebrews 11:1;
Romans 3:22–24; 2 Corinthians 5:21

God's Promises

"Behold, the days are coming," says the LORD, "that I will raise to David a Branch of righteousness; a King shall reign and prosper, and execute judgment and righteousness in the earth. In His days Judah will be saved, and Israel will dwell safely; now this is His name by which He will be called: THE LORD OUR RIGHTEOUSNESS." (Jer. 23:5–6)

I will greatly rejoice in the LORD, my soul shall be joyful in my God; for He has clothed me with the garments of salvation, He has covered me with the robe of righteousness, as a bridegroom decks himself with ornaments, and as a bride adorns herself with her jewels. (Isa. 61:10)

He made Him who knew no sin to be sin for us, that we might become the righteousness of God in Him. (2 Cor. 5:21)

He restores my soul; He leads me in the paths of righteousness for His name's sake. (Ps. 23:3)

Sow for yourselves righteousness; reap in mercy; break up your fallow ground, for it is time to seek the LORD, till He comes and rains righteousness on you. (Hos. 10:12)

My Prayer

Heavenly Father, my righteousness, thank You for making me righteous in Your sight and enabling me to walk by faith and not by sight. What a blessed gift You have provided me through the sacrificial death and resurrection of Your Son, Jesus Christ. I admit that I am a sinner and cannot restore myself. I need You in my life, Lord. I repent of trying to do things on my own. My attempts are so fallible. You have restored my soul through Christ's shed blood, and I believe that You will also restore my soul to keep You in the center. I drive a stake in the ground today and say no to fear and yes to faith! I will walk forward in faith, fully trusting You for the outcomes of my needs. You are my righteousness, and wherever You lead, I will follow. In Jesus' name I pray. Amen.

2 Corinthians 5:21; 1 Peter 2:24

My Worship

Savior, like a shepherd lead us,
Much we need Thy tender care;
In Thy pleasant pastures feed us,
For our use, Thy folds prepare.

Blessed Jesus, blessed Jesus!
Thou hast bought us, Thine we are.
Blessed Jesus, blessed Jesus!
Thou hast bought us, Thine we are.

We are Thine, do thou befriend us,
Be the guardian of our way;
Keep Thy flock, from sin defend us,
Seek us when we go astray.

Blessed Jesus, blessed Jesus!
Hear, O hear, us when we pray.
Blessed Jesus, blessed Jesus!
Hear, O hear, us when we pray.

Thou hast promised to receive us,
Poor and sinful though we be;
Thou hast mercy to relieve us,
Grace to cleanse and pow'r to free.

Blessed Jesus, blessed Jesus!
Early let us turn to Thee.
Blessed Jesus, blessed Jesus!
Early let us turn to Thee.

> Early let us seek Thy favor,
> Early let us do Thy will;
> Blessed Lord and only Savior,
> With Thy love our beings fill.
>
> Blessed Jesus, blessed Jesus!
> Thou hast loved us, love us still.
> Blessed Jesus, blessed Jesus!
> Thou hast loved us, love us still.[14]

Reflection and Realignment

What unknown might you be facing? Write down the date and the decision that is before you. Now pray, asking the Lord to lead you to the right path. If your answer does not come immediately, keep waiting on the Lord with prayerful attention to what He is saying to your heart. Trust God to provide you with the answer at just the right time. When He does, go back to your written statement and write the answer He gave you and the date He gave it. He is faithful!

DAY 15

I AM
Your Master

Prior to this season of immobilization, your life was so busy with activity that you neglected to nurture your heart. You were living in a frenzy. This self-imposed busyness devoured your time and distracted you from Me. Even before you were out of bed each morning, you were calculating your to-do list for the day. Anxiety filled your heart as you approached sunrise. You burned the late-night candle and then rose early the next day so you could get everything accomplished. But I am *Adonai*, your Master and majestic Lord. As you submit yourself to Me and My restful ways, I will secure your footing so that you will be able to climb high hills without difficulty.

You have forgotten the most important thing: nourishing your soul. The call of the urgent interferes with your call from Me. Oh, My child, this is not My desire for you. Your busyness has been your drug of choice. It produced a feeling of productivity and gave you a sense of value and accomplishment, but this was all an illusion. While on the outside it appeared that you had it all together, your soul was suffering. Though you filled your life with many good things, you neglected the best.

I want you to take an inward journey—a journey of the heart. This journey involves giving up your activities and agendas for the sake of nurturing the core of who you are. Do not neglect using this time to invest in your relationship with Me. I deeply care about you and desire to see you healthy and whole.

As *Adonai*, your Lord and Master, I call you Mine. I make your crooked places straight and your rough places smooth. I provide you with sure footing through life's troubles. I created you, and I know all about you and desire to be intimately involved in every area of your life. With loving-kindness I have drawn you, and with loving-kindness I will build you back up. Do not let life master you. Instead, master it by allowing Me to be your Master. Your busyness has depleted you, and it has also stolen from you peaceful moments in My presence. Resolve today to clear your mind and unclutter your heart, creating a new discipline—that of being still. This is where deep soul healing is found.

The tyranny of the urgent will always battle for your attention and try to steal your sanity. Settle your thoughts on My presence and savor the sweetness of My satisfying Word. As My promises penetrate your innermost being, they will become like the oxygen you breathe. Breathe deeply, My child. This is your pathway to peace.

Isaiah 6:1; Psalm 18:33; Ezekiel 16:8; Isaiah 40:4; Habakkuk 3:19; Jeremiah 31:3–4

God's Promises

Thus says the LORD God, the Holy One of Israel: "In returning and rest you shall be saved; in quietness and confidence shall be your strength." (Isa. 30:15)

My soul waits for the Lord more than those who watch for the morning—yes, more than those who watch for the morning. (Ps. 130:6)

The LORD God is my strength; He will make my feet like deer's feet, and He will make me walk on my high hills. (Hab. 3:19)

My Prayer

Heavenly Father, my Master and majestic Lord, how excellent is Your name in all the earth. You who have set Your glory above the heavens have also ordained strength to those who trust in You. When I consider the heavens and the handiwork of Your hands, the moon and stars that You have divinely placed in their locations, I am humbled. For You have created the world and all that is in it, and yet You still desire to nurture my heart. Please forgive me for heeding the tyranny of the urgent and dismissing Your invitation to be still. I want to exchange my busyness for Your blessing. I want to trade my chaos for Your constancy. You are always with me, and Your divine guidance and grace will see me through this time. In Jesus' name I pray. Amen.

Psalm 8:1–2; Joshua 1:9

My Worship

When the shadows thickly gather,
Clouding all thy onward way,
Think not what shall be tomorrow;
Seek God's help just for today.

Step by step He leads me onward,
Step by step the way reveals;
But what in the future lieth,
In His mercy He conceals.

Should the coming days bring burdens,
Or be fraught with grief or care,
Trust Him in the hour of trial;
He will make thee strong to bear.

Daily strength He ever giveth,
For each day rich grace bestows;
And each morrow, as it dawneth,
Still His loving-kindness shows.

Then why should we shrink or falter
When the onward path looks dim,
Knowing light will never fail us
While we walk by faith with Him?[15]

Reflection and Realignment

Yielding to God as our Master and Lord requires us to adjust. Prayerfully consider whether you need to let go of certain things in your life. Ask God to make clear to you what He wants you to give over to Him, and ask Him to help you do it. Share your prayer with a trusted friend or family member so they can pray alongside you as you leave this matter with God.

DAY 16

I AM

THE ONE TRUE GOD

My child, in this difficult time you cannot make sense of your present weakness. You question My presence with you and My promises for you, and you feel as if I am nowhere to be found. Oh, My precious child, do not allow your doubts to confuse your thinking. I am *El Elohei Yisra'el*, the God of Israel, who is holy and distinct from all other gods. Yet I am the God of your life as well. I am for you, not against you, and I desire a growing relationship with you.

There is nothing the enemy would like more than to make you think My presence is absent when you need it most. When doubts swell up, resist them, and draw near to Me. "Be still, and know that I am God." I am with you. I am for you. I will never leave you or abandon you. You feel as if your prayers are hitting the ceiling, but they really are penetrating My heart. The confidence you need during this time of confusion will come from believing My Word: if you ask anything according to My will, I will hear you and answer you. Even when you do not have the words to pray, My Spirit intercedes on your behalf with groanings that cannot be uttered.

I am presently working behind the scenes of your life for your future good. You cannot fathom this right now; the dark clouds surrounding you have obscured your view. But your sight will clear if you see your condition through My eyes—eyes of faith. Trust Me, My child, through all the uncertainties before you. Refuse to let worry consume you, and take this moment to seek My face. Cast all your cares upon Me, for I care for you. I am your hope, your help, and your shield.

There is no other God like Me. Even when your circumstances do not make sense, I still make sense, and I am in control. "I will go before you and make the crooked places straight; I will break in pieces the gates of bronze and cut the bars of iron. I will give you the treasures of darkness and hidden riches of secret places, that you may know that I, the LORD, who call you by your name, am the God of Israel." The valley before you is deep, but My love is deeper. Hold on to My love and the comfort it brings. Walk with Me, and allow My whispers of love to still your aching soul. I will not fail you or let you go.

The time has come for you to take your stand—and lean on Me like never before! What will you choose? Will you live this day in doubt or in faith?

Genesis 33:19–20; John 17:3; Psalm 46:10; Isaiah 41:10; Romans 8:31; Deuteronomy 31:8; 1 John 5:14–15; Romans 8:26, 28; 1 Peter 5:7; 1 Peter 1:3; Psalm 33:20; Isaiah 45:2–5; Psalm 73:23–26

GOD'S PROMISES

The LORD is the true God; He is the living God and the everlasting King. (Jer. 10:10)

This is eternal life, that they may know You, the only true God, and Jesus Christ whom You have sent. (John 17:3)

Assuredly, I say to you, whoever says to this mountain, "Be removed and be cast into the sea," and does not doubt in his heart, but believes that those things he says will be done, he will have whatever he says. (Mark 11:23)

This is the confidence that we have in Him, that if we ask anything according to His will, He hears us. And if we know that He hears us, whatever we ask, we know that we have the petitions that we have asked of Him. (1 John 5:14–15)

The Spirit also helps in our weaknesses. For we do not know what we should pray for as we ought, but the Spirit Himself makes intercession for us with groanings which cannot be uttered. (Rom. 8:26)

My Prayer

Heavenly Father, You are the Lord God of Israel, distinct and separate from all gods, yet You are the God of my life as well, and You desire a close relationship with me. Help me stop striving and start receiving—receiving more of You and Your presence in my life. I have been trying to do things in my own strength and power, as the Israelites did when they walked through the wilderness. But You remained faithful to them, and I thank You for Your faithfulness to me as well. I repent of trying to control the situations in my life. I choose now to release my angst and let You reign in my heart, my mind, my emotions. I give all my doubts, worries, and fears to You and trust You for all outcomes. Your Word says that perfect love casts out all fear, and today I rest in Your perfect love. Thank You, Lord God, for not giving up on me but for pursuing me and lavishing Your love upon me today. In Jesus' name I pray. Amen.

Genesis 33:19–20; Jeremiah 10:10; Zechariah 4:6; 2 Timothy 2:13; 1 John 4:18

My Worship

O Love that wilt not let me go,
I rest my weary soul in Thee;
I give thee back the life I owe,
That in thine ocean depths its flow
May richer, fuller be.

O Light that follow'st all my way,
I yield my flick'ring torch to Thee;
My heart restores its borrowed ray,
That in Thy sunshine's blaze its day
May brighter, fairer be.

O Joy that seekest me through pain,
I cannot close my heart to Thee;
I trace the rainbow through the rain
And feel the promise is not vain
That morn shall tearless be.

O cross that liftest up my head,
I dare not ask to fly from thee;
I lay in dust life's glory dead,
And from the ground there blossoms red
Life that shall endless be.[16]

Reflection and Realignment

In which areas of your life are you struggling to trust God? Take some time to sit still and ponder why that may be. List those areas, and date them with today's date. Next to each area write, "Lord God, God over Israel and God over my life, I trust You with _____." Choose one of God's promises to claim over each area of your life in which trusting God has become difficult for you.

DAY 17

I AM
Your Sanctuary

The many concerns you hold within your heart are affecting your thought life. Worries about your future, your health, and your happiness saturate your soul with apprehension and anxiety. You question the state of this world and the details of your life, yet you neglect the state of your own mind, which has become increasingly negative. You don't realize it, but your negative thoughts deter you from embracing My goodness. If you want lasting change in your life, you need to start by changing your thinking. You do this by turning Your thoughts to Me—your safe place, your sanctuary, the solace for your soul amidst the chaos and confusion of this world.

Train your mind to pay attention to what you are thinking about. When negative thoughts come into your mind, exchange them immediately for thoughts focused on Me. Receive into your mind only those thoughts that are true, noble, right, pure, lovely, admirable, excellent, and praiseworthy. These kinds of thoughts honor Me and will produce the fruit of peace in your life.

Your mind is the control center of your body and your emotions. The enemy knows that if he can sabotage your thinking, he can sabotage your whole being. Choose today to stop allowing negative thoughts to consume your thinking, and start receiving only those thoughts that edify and encourage your soul. The renewing of your mind is a discipline you must practice daily. It involves just as much putting off your old negative thinking patterns as putting on new, edifying ways of thinking. Doing this today may not change your thinking immediately, but doing it daily will transform your thinking over time.

The only way to be fully released from the death grip of defeatist thinking is to keep your thoughts firmly fixed upon Me. Run to Me, and receive your rest. Seek Me, and be sustained with My songs of deliverance. Trust in Me, and see your fears exchanged for faith. I have unlimited power, and I am sovereign over and in control of all things.

Just as I was with Gideon, so I will be with you. Faulty thinking consumed Gideon's mind—he didn't consider himself capable of delivering Israel from the hand of Midian. But My presence revealed otherwise to him. I knew he was from the weakest clan in his tribe, and I deliberately chose him so My power could be manifested through his weakness. As I have assured you before, in My hands even those who feel most inadequate are equipped. You don't need to feel strong to be effective. I am your strength, and when you are weak, then I am strong. You see, this is how I work. I delight in using the weak things of this world to demonstrate My power. Recall to your mind the wonders I have done, the miracles I have initiated through the ages by the stroke of My almighty hand. Changed hearts and transformed lives are My specialty. As you seek Me and surrender to My ways, I will bring you out of your flawed thinking and into the promised land of My peace.

Jeremiah 17:12; 2 Corinthians 10:5; Philippians 4:8; Matthew 11:28; Psalm 32:7; Psalm 56:3–4; Job 36:22; Colossians 1:16; Judges 6:15–16; 2 Corinthians 12:11; 1 Corinthians 1:27

God's Promises

The LORD of hosts, Him you shall hallow; let Him be your fear, and let Him be your dread. He will be as a sanctuary. (Isa. 8:13–14)

Even the sparrow has found a home, and the swallow a nest for herself, where she may lay her young—even Your altars, O LORD of hosts, my King and my God. (Ps. 84:3)

Whatever things are true, whatever things are noble, whatever things are just, whatever things are pure, whatever things are lovely, whatever things are of good report, if there is any virtue and if there is anything praiseworthy—meditate on these things. The things which you learned and received and heard and saw in me, these do, and the God of peace will be with you. (Phil. 4:8–9)

My Prayer

Heavenly Father, thank You for being my sanctuary—a safe place where I can go and have my mind renewed. I praise Your glorious name. You are forgiving and good, abundant in mercy, and abounding in love. You are the One who lifts my head, brightens my countenance, and extends Your faithfulness to me and all my future generations. Your promises never fail. When I am afraid, I can trust in You. When the cares and concerns of this world confront me and tempt me toward a negative mind-set, my soul can find rest in Your peaceful presence. Exert Your authority in my life and over all my needs, and let me not be consumed by my own futile thinking. I desire to have Your thoughts, oh God, and want more of You in my life. In Jesus' name I pray. Amen.

Psalm 86:5; Psalm 3:3; Psalm 18:28; Psalm 100:5; Psalm 56:3

My Worship

Like a river glorious is God's perfect peace,
Over all victorious in its bright increase.
Perfect, yet it floweth fuller every day;
Perfect, yet it groweth deeper all the way.

Stayed upon Jehovah, hearts are fully blest,
Finding, as He promised, perfect peace and rest.

Hidden in the hollow of His blessed hand,
Never foe can follow, never traitor stand.
Not a surge of worry, not a shade of care,
Not a blast of hurry touch the spirit there.

Every joy or trial falleth from above,
Traced upon our dial by the Sun of love;
We may trust Him fully all for us to do;
They who trust Him wholly find Him wholly true.[17]

Reflection and Realignment

Take some time to examine the thoughts that most fill your mind. As each thought comes to mind, ask yourself, *Is this thought a peace-giving, edifying, soul-nurturing thought? Or is it full of condemnation, negativity, fear, or shame?* If it is the latter, dismiss the thought, and exchange it with one of God's promises.

DAY 18

I AM
Your Strength

You are continuing to bear a burden of unforgiveness. Without realizing it, you have become in bondage to those who have wounded you. Even though some of this pain was caused years ago, and you have given it to Me before, the negative words and hurtful actions that sliced your soul in two are coming back to your mind. My child, I see the ongoing struggle to fully forgive, and I will help you. For I am *El*, the strong One, and I keep My promises and show mercy for a thousand generations to those who love and obey Me. No problem is too great for Me to resolve and no obstacle too high for Me to overcome.

As the Almighty God, you can depend upon Me for everything. I am your strength and your song, and I have also become your salvation. It is not your place to vindicate yourself for the wrongs done against you or to prove to anyone that you are right. Do what is right, and give your hurts over to Me. My Son, Jesus Christ, is your greatest advocate. It is He who will defend and plead your case. The enemy has put you on trial, but My Son will stand strong on your behalf. He will intercede and fight for you.

But you have a part that you must play, and that is to forgive. Extending forgiveness does not mean that you no longer remember the offenses done against you. Extending forgiveness means that you choose to not dwell on those offenses anymore. It means that you let go of your offender and let Me take control.

When you extend forgiveness, it signifies that I have freely forgiven you and given you the ability to freely forgive others. This is because when you confess your sin to Me, I cast it into the deepest ocean of My love, where it is remembered no more. This pure, perfect love provides you with the ability to forgive the person who has hurt you. Instead of being burdened by bitterness, embrace the blessings of My love, and be set free!

Deuteronomy 7:9; Exodus 15:2; 1 John 2:1; Hebrews 7:25;
Colossians 3:13; 1 John 1:9; 1 Corinthians 13:4–8

God's Promises

My flesh and my heart fail; but God is the strength of my heart and my portion forever. (Ps. 73:26)

God is my strength and power, and He makes my way perfect. (2 Sam. 22:33)

Be kind to one another, tenderhearted, forgiving one another, even as God in Christ forgave you. (Eph. 4:32)

As the elect of God, holy and beloved, put on tender mercies, kindness, humility, meekness, longsuffering; bearing with one another, and forgiving one another, if anyone has a complaint against another; even as Christ forgave you, so you also must do. (Col. 3:12–13)

My Prayer

Father God, the strong One, thank You for Your power to overcome all obstacles. I know I can depend on You for everything, even for the strength and ability to forgive those who have deeply wounded me. Thank You for extending Your forgiveness to me, and now I in turn forgive all those who have hurt me. I place my offenders on Your altar and ask You to bless them. I repent of my wrong thinking and negativity toward them. Help me see them with fresh, new eyes. Help me to stop obsessing over their faults and to find the good in them. Cleanse my mind of all the painful memories, and fill me with Your compassion so I may be a blessing to someone today. In Jesus' name I pray. Amen.

1 John 1:9; Ephesians 4:32; Colossians 3:12

My Worship

When my will is weak,
My thinking confused,
My conscience burdened with guilt,
I must remember,
Choose to believe,
Your love for me won't fail.

God of compassion,
Shine Your light on me;
Show me the healing
You want me to see.
Take my sorrow,

Turn it to joy once again;
Give me a changed heart, O God.
Give me a changed heart, O God.

When I feel abandoned, misunderstood,
Walking through this world alone,
I must remember,
Choose to believe,
Your love for me is always there.[18]

REFLECTION AND REALIGNMENT

Who might you be struggling to forgive? What offenses against you tempt you to spiral into a pit of bitter emotions? Make a list of any people who have offended you and the offenses they have committed against you. Next to each person write today's date and the words "Released and forgiven." Then pray, asking God to help you release the offense and forgive each offender just as Jesus would do.

DAY 19

I AM
Your Creator

My child, you have allowed the chattering voices of naysayers to consume the treasures of your heart. Their critical words over the years have wounded your spirit and now, as you lie incapacitated, they bounce more loudly than ever in the caverns of your mind. These words have caused you to doubt the dreams I have planted in your heart, impeding your progress. Do not digest their judgments and negativity. Look to Me, and listen for My voice. I am your *Elohim*, the all-powerful Creator of the universe and of your life. I know all, I see all, and I am with you at all times. When I formed you, I formed you with a purpose—a purpose that includes so much more than you can ever imagine.

The naysayers do not know your potential. By allowing their voices to frame your thinking, your energy has been zapped, and you have lost your zeal. The onslaught of their attacks against you has hindered your enthusiasm and stolen your joy like the crashing waves that erode the sands of the seashore. Your fervor and enthusiasm have fizzled out. Do not allow the discouraging opinions of others to stifle the growth I am trying to bring about within you, but take confidence and comfort in who I am and what I can do. "Keep your heart with all diligence, for out of it spring the issues of life."

As you gaze upon the starry night sky, keep in mind that the God who set the stars in place is the same God who now walks with you. Your cynics will only distract you from completely grasping the wonders I have prepared for you. Their voices are like barricades, hedging you in hopelessness. But My voice is the bridge that brings you to hope. For I am about to do something new. Can you see it? Soon it will burst forth. I will make a pathway through the wilderness and create rivers in the desert of your difficulties. Your current adversities are nothing compared to the vast expanse of My blessings that are coming. Persevere through these trials, My child, for they are producing a depth of character in you that will cause you to shine.

Genesis 1:1–3; Psalm 139:13–14; Ephesians 3:20; Proverbs 4:23; Isaiah 43:19; Colossians 1:11–12

God's Promises

In the beginning God created the heavens and the earth. The earth was without form, and void; and darkness was on the face of the deep. And the Spirit of God was hovering over the face of the waters. Then God said, "Let there be light"; and there was light. (Gen. 1:1–3)

[He] is able to do exceedingly abundantly above all that we ask or think, according to the power that works in us. (Eph. 3:20)

Behold, I will do a new thing, now it shall spring forth; shall you not know it? I will even make a road in the wilderness and rivers in the desert. (Isa. 43:19)

My Prayer

Father God, Creator and sustainer of the world and all that is in it, I praise Your great name and thank You for revealing Yourself to me. I am humbled by Your presence and so thankful for Your intimate care and concern for me. You are not an unreachable God who created the world and then abandoned it, but You are an intimate God who is with me and cares about every detail of my life. Thank You for manifesting Your love to me by giving me an example of courage in Your Son, Jesus Christ. Fully God, Jesus came to Earth to live as a man. He encountered the same adversities I encounter, yet He knew no sin and did not use His adversities as an excuse to sin or strike back. Thank You for Christ's example and how He jumped into the darkness to bring forth light. Even through all the ridicule and rejection He faced, He kept His focus on His mission, His ears attentive to Your voice, and His eyes fixed on Your presence. Please help me, Lord God, to do the same. In Jesus' name I pray. Amen.

Isaiah 41:10; Matthew 10:30–31

My Worship

Come, thou fount of every blessing,
Tune my heart to sing Thy grace;
Streams of mercy, never ceasing,
Call for songs of loudest praise.
Teach me some melodious sonnet
Sung by flaming tongues above.
Praise the mount! I'm fixed upon it,
Mount of God's unchanging love.

Here I raise mine Ebenezer;
Hither by Thy help I'm come;
And I hope, by Thy good pleasure,
Safely to arrive at home.
Jesus sought me when a stranger,
Wandering from the fold of God;
He, to rescue me from danger,
Interposed His precious blood.

O to grace how great a debtor
Daily I'm constrained to be!
Let Thy goodness, like a fetter,
Bind my wand'ring heart to thee.
Prone to wander, Lord, I feel it,
Prone to leave the God I love;
Here's my heart, O take and seal it,
Seal it for Thy courts above.[19]

REFLECTION AND REALIGNMENT

How have the judgments of naysayers framed your thinking? In what ways have critical, fault-finding words sabotaged your ability to clearly hear God's voice? It is time to dismiss the voices of the naysayers and receive your peace in the knowledge that God created you, and He did so for a purpose. Write down the promise of God in today's reading that was most meaningful to you, and memorize this verse over the next week.

DAY 20

I AM
Your Rock

As you approach what seem like the great waves of the Red Sea, remember that I am greater. Your inability to care for your family as you did before is requiring new arrangements, and you are faced with difficult decisions. These challenges seem insurmountable, but in the same way I led the Israelites through the sea-raging pathway, so I will lead you. For I am your *Yahweh Tzur*, your rock, and there is none like Me. I am your stability and support through life's storms. My solid foundation absorbs the blows of the battering waves.

Do not allow your doubt and fear to keep you from stepping into uncharted waters. Stand strong in Me. The moment your faith is activated, My power will be manifested. Take one small step at a time, and I will secure your footing.

Do not allow the storm's giant form or ferocity to distract you. Keep your eyes firmly fixed on Me, and I will lead you and guide you. My steadfast love is your stabilizer and will strongly support you through every trial. Call to mind who I am, apply My promises to your areas of need, and watch what I will do. I am preparing the stage for your deliverance, working diligently behind the scenes to orchestrate every detail.

Seek Me while I may be found. Call upon Me while I am near. I do not want you to walk through this sea-raging pathway alone. Lean on Me, and find your strength. I will hold you up, and I will hem you in. Trust Me, My child, for those who trust in Me are as Mount Zion, which cannot be moved.

1 Samuel 2:2; Psalm 31:3; Isaiah 55:6; Psalm 125:1

God's Promises

He is the Rock, His work is perfect; for all His ways are justice, a God of truth and without injustice; righteous and upright is He. (Deut. 32:4)

The LORD is my rock and my fortress and my deliverer; my God, my strength, in whom I will trust; my shield and the horn of my salvation, my stronghold. I will call upon the LORD, who is worthy to be praised; so shall I be saved from my enemies. (Ps. 18:2–3)

They remembered that God was their rock, and the Most High God their Redeemer. (Ps. 78:35)

In You, O LORD, I put my trust; let me never be ashamed; deliver me in Your righteousness. Bow down Your ear to me, deliver me speedily; be my rock of refuge, a fortress of defense to save me. For You are my rock and my fortress; therefore, for Your name's sake, lead me and guide me. (Ps. 31:1–3)

My Prayer

Heavenly Father, thank You for being my rock, the One I can fully depend upon. Though my life is filled with much uncertainty, You, oh God, are my strength and support. You will shelter me from the storm. In You I put my trust, and I am kept safe. Thank You for having Your eyes always upon me and Your ears fully attentive to my cries. Though my distresses are many, I will trust You, knowing full well that all outcomes are in Your hands. Because of Your loving-kindness I will not be consumed. Your compassions are continual and greet me each morning, and Your faithfulness is ever so great. In Jesus' name I pray. Amen.

Isaiah 25:4; Proverbs 29:25; Psalm 34:15; Lamentations 3:22–23

My Worship

Rock of ages, cleft for me,
Let me hide myself in Thee;
Let the water and the blood,
From Thy wounded side which flowed,
Be of sin the double cure,
Save from wrath and make me pure.

Could my tears forever flow,
Could my zeal no languor know,
These for sin could not atone,
Thou must save, and Thou alone.
In my hand no price I bring;
Simply to Thy cross I cling.

While I draw this fleeting breath,
When mine eyes shall close in death,
When I rise to worlds unknown,
And behold Thee on Thy throne,
Rock of ages, cleft for me,
Let me hide myself in Thee.[20]

Reflection and Realignment

What overwhelming ordeal lies before you? Write out a prayer inviting God, your rock, to be your strength and support, your shelter and security through this time of storm.

DAY 21

I AM
Your Forgiving Father

My child, you are precious to Me. Even before you were born, I knew you. The very breath you breathe is evidence that I am working in your life. I know every hair on your head, and I have your name engraved on the palm of My hand. Despite knowing all this, you live under a heavy weight of condemnation, enslaved to the voices in your memory that say you aren't good enough. Like a prisoner behind locked bars, you have not entered into your full freedom. I am not a harsh taskmaster who loves you only for what you can do. I am your forgiving Father, and I love you for who you are. I do not hold any wrongs against you but delight in showing you mercy. I have cast your sins into the depths of the sea and remember them no more. Yes, no more!

You are not a mistake, a blunder, or a mishap. You were given life for a tailor-made purpose, and you were created to fulfill a personal plan. See, My thoughts toward you are always good, and My love for you will never end. My love is eternal, abundantly given, and I never withhold it for any reason. Though at times you drift from Me, I continue to pursue you and pour My deepest affections upon you. I accept you just the way you are and rejoice over you on your good days as well as on your bad ones.

Push the bars of your prison open. Your independence day has come! "Though your sins are like scarlet, they shall be as white as snow; though they are red like crimson, they shall be as wool." Like a waterfall that washes away the impurities in the stream below, so My forgiveness washes away the impurities of your soul. Confess your sins, and be cleansed. Receive from Me, and rest. My forgiveness is more than enough for your cleansing. Do not look to others for this affirmation—look to Me. You are treasured. You are loved. You are forgiven. You are Mine. Return to Me, for I have redeemed you. Your time of refreshing has come.

Jeremiah 1:5; Job 33:4; Luke 12:7; Isaiah 49:16; Isaiah 43:1; Micah 7:18–19; Hebrews 10:17; Psalm 139:13–14; Ephesians 2:10; Jeremiah 29:11; Psalm 139:17; 1 Corinthians 13:8; Psalm 66:20; Zephaniah 3:17; Isaiah 1:18; 1 John 1:9; Isaiah 44:22; Acts 3:19

God's Promises

Grace, mercy, and peace will be with you from God the Father and from the Lord Jesus Christ, the Son of the Father, in truth and love. (2 John 1:3)

You are God, ready to pardon, gracious and merciful, slow to anger, abundant in kindness. (Neh. 9:17)

You did not receive the spirit of bondage again to fear, but you received the Spirit of adoption by whom we cry out, "Abba, Father." (Rom. 8:15)

I, even I, am He who blots out your transgressions for My own sake; and I will not remember your sins. (Isa. 43:25)

Behold what manner of love the Father has bestowed on us, that we should be called children of God! (1 John 3:1)

My Prayer

Forgiving Father, thank You for forgiving me. I repent of the ways in which I have drifted from You, shrinking back from You because I thought You were condemning me. Bring me back, oh God. Restore to me the joy of Your salvation, and uphold me by Your Holy Spirit. Help me know and accept Your love for me so I can love You in return with all my heart, soul, strength, and mind and love my neighbor as myself. Lord, I cannot do anything without You, but with You I can do all things. Instead of feeling condemnation from You or others, help me have compassion on people and be able to love even those who are most difficult to love. In You I can stand secure. Thank You for gracing me with Your goodness, oh God, and presenting me faultless before the presence of Your glory with exceeding joy. In Jesus' name I pray. Amen.

Ephesians 4:32; Matthew 15:8; Psalm 51:12; Luke 10:27; Philippians 4:13; Jude 1:24

My Worship

Redeemed, how I love to proclaim it!
Redeemed by the blood of the Lamb!
Redeemed through His infinite mercy—
His child, and forever, I am.

Redeemed, redeemed, redeemed by the blood of the Lamb!
Redeemed, redeemed, His child, and forever, I am.

Redeemed and so happy in Jesus,
No language my rapture can tell!
I know that the light of His presence
With me doth continually dwell.

I think of my blessed Redeemer;
I think of Him all the day long.
I sing for I cannot be silent;
His love is the theme of my song.

I know I shall see in His beauty
The King in whose law I delight,
Who lovingly guardeth my footsteps
And giveth me songs in the night.[21]

Reflection and Realignment

When has condemnation weighed you down? What past memories haunt you? Cast these cares upon the Lord, and ask the Holy Spirit to guide your thoughts as you meditate on Romans 8:1: "There is therefore now no condemnation to those who are in Christ Jesus."

DAY 22

I AM
Your Light

On rainy days when life is dull, My light seems dimmed by clouds of indifference and difficulties. In this dark place you have believed lies of the enemy and become downcast. But My love for you is still present. Stay close to Me, My child, for I am your light, and you need not fear. I will lead you. The adversities you have encountered are overwhelming to you. They have left you exhausted and ready to give up, but I will help you persevere as you lean on Me. Remember, this battle is not yours but Mine. The light of My presence goes with you, and it will illuminate the path before you.

I have made this day just for you. As you experience the warmth of the sun's rays, let it remind you of the warmth of My love. Though it seems as if My love is most present on sunny days, when life is going well and My light is most radiant, My love is also present on the rainy days. This is because My love is constant. It is always present and available, but you must take time to see it, because it is visible only to those who look for it.

As your journey unfolds, I am teaching you to be more conscious of My love and My light. But in order to do this, I need your full attention. The hardships you have encountered have dulled your senses, but as you travel through this time of testing, I am training you to look at life through My light-filled lens.

But there is still work for you to do: the work of investigating the dark chambers of your soul. You have allowed these places to go unattended for too long. Now it is time for you to take an inward journey to expose the lies you have believed. Like a miner searching for coal, use My light to pinpoint those areas of your soul that have fallen prey to the accusations of the enemy. Do not allow the darkness of the mineshaft to deter you from completing this work. This pursuit will require you to stay focused on My light. As you do, the light will penetrate the darkest areas of your heart and lead to great discovery. "For you were once darkness, but now you are light in the Lord. Walk as children of light."

The entrance of My words gives light; it gives understanding to the simple. Stay within the scope of My light, child. Let it guide your every step. This is your pathway to victory.

Psalm 27:1; Isaiah 48:17; 2 Chronicles 20:15; Psalm 118:24; Exodus 34:6; Ephesians 5:8; Psalm 119:130

God's Promises

The LORD is my light and my salvation; whom shall I fear? The LORD is the strength of my life; of whom shall I be afraid? (Ps. 27:1)

In Him was life, and the life was the light of men. And the light shines in the darkness, and the darkness did not comprehend it. (John 1:4–5)

Arise, shine; for your light has come! And the glory of the LORD is risen upon you. (Isa. 60:1)

> If we walk in the light as He is in the light, we have fellowship with one another, and the blood of Jesus Christ His Son cleanses us from all sin. (1 John 1:7)

My Prayer

Heavenly Father, thank You for being my light. In You there is no darkness at all. As I journey inside my soul, shine Your truth into those areas in which I have believed lies. Lord, as Your child of light, I will walk in Your light and reclaim the territory of my soul stolen by the enemy. Today I proclaim that You, oh God, have delivered me from the domain of darkness and positioned me in the kingdom of Your glorious light, where all things hidden have now been revealed and I can walk in open fellowship with You, my light and my Lord. What freedom! What joy! I praise Your name, oh God, for pulling me out of the pit and giving me a new place to stand. From this day forward I will walk in the light and have nothing in common with darkness. Help me shine my light before all men so they may see my good works and glorify You, my Father in heaven. In Jesus' name I pray. Amen.

Colossians 1:13; Psalm 40:2; Matthew 5:16

My Worship

> And can it be that I should gain
> An interest in the Savior's blood?
> Died He for me, who caused His pain?

For me, who Him to death pursued?
Amazing love! How can it be
That Thou, my God, shouldst die for me?
Amazing love! How can it be
That Thou, my God, shouldst die for me?

He left His Father's throne above,
So free, so infinite His grace!
Emptied Himself of all but love
And bled for Adam's helpless race.
'Tis mercy all, immense and free,
For, O my God, it found out me!
'Tis mercy all, immense and free,
For, O my God, it found out me!

Long my imprisoned spirit lay
Fast bound in sin and nature's night.
Thine eye diffused a quickening ray.
I woke; the dungeon flamed with light!
My chains fell off; my heart was free.
I rose, went forth, and followed Thee.
My chains fell off; my heart was free.
I rose, went forth, and followed Thee.

No condemnation now I dread;
Jesus, and all in Him, is mine!
Alive in Him, my living head,
And clothed in righteousness divine,
Bold I approach the eternal throne
And claim the crown through Christ, my own.
Bold I approach the eternal throne
And claim the crown through Christ, my own.[22]

Reflection and Realignment

Write down the words "I am a child of light. I am a child of light. Hallelujah, I am a child of light!" Now say the words aloud, and then meditate on Ephesians 5:8: "You were once darkness, but now you are light in the Lord. Walk as children of light." During your time of reflection and meditation, ask God to guide you to walk as His child of light and to help you discern what that looks like for you.

DAY 23

I AM
YOUR REFUGE

You are disturbed by injustices you have endured. They grip your heart and cut your soul like a knife. The world is not fair. Life is not fair. You feel torn, and the tempest within your soul burns as you ponder all the wrongs. Take cover in Me, for I am your *Machaseh*, your refuge, and I will enable you to face your fears. I am here. As your shield, I will protect you. As your deliverer, I will resurrect you. I see and know all that you are encountering, and I care.

Your indignation has you tied up in knots. You do not know what to do or where to turn. You have so many unanswered questions, and the rage within you roars. All this has blurred your focus. My child, turn your eyes back to Me, and trust Me to work all these things out for the good. Though everything within you wants to fight back against the wrongs, don't forget that the battle is Mine, not yours.

Take a moment to exhale. Breathe in My peace as you breathe out the anxieties of your soul. Though your life is hedged with uncertainty, I am your constant security. I do not change; I am infinitely the same. So find refuge in Me, as My prophet Elijah did. After he prayed and brought fire down from heaven to consume a water-soaked sacrifice, showing My might and that I am indeed the one true God, Elijah fled in fear and frustration from the wicked Queen Jezebel. Yet I didn't scold him or expect him to stand strong; I gently confronted him through an angel sent to minister to his needs. Then, as he hid in a remote cave, I manifested My almighty presence and power to him through My still small voice.

My child, if need be, take cover for a time. You are weary and worn. During this season of solitude, find your replenishment in Me. For I am your refuge, and I will revive you. Trust Me, and look up, My child. Keep praying. I have a plan that extends beyond the cares of this chaotic time.

Psalm 91:2; Romans 8:28; 1 Samuel 17:47; Malachi 3:6;
1 Kings 18:38–39; 1 Kings 19:11–12

God's Promises

I will say of the LORD, "He is my refuge and my fortress; my God, in Him I will trust." (Ps. 91:2)

You have been a strength to the poor, a strength to the needy in his distress, a refuge from the storm, a shade from the heat; for the blast of the terrible ones is as a storm against the wall. (Isa. 25:4)

God is our refuge and strength, a very present help in trouble. Therefore we will not fear, even though the earth be removed, and though the mountains be carried into the midst of the sea; though its waters roar and be troubled, though the mountains shake with its swelling. (Ps. 46:1–3)

I will lift up my eyes to the hills—from whence comes my help? My help comes from the LORD, who made heaven and earth. (Ps. 121:1–2)

The LORD also will be a refuge for the oppressed, a refuge in times of trouble. And those who know Your name will put their trust in You; for You, LORD, have not forsaken those who seek You. (Ps. 9:9–10)

MY PRAYER

Heavenly Father, thank You for being my refuge. Even amid the flood of great waters, I will not be consumed. For You are my hiding place, oh God, and will preserve me from trouble. You surround me with songs of deliverance and keep me safe. Thank You that in the midst of trying times, You are there. You promise to instruct me and teach me in the way I should go. You will guide me in Your truth and teach me, for You are God, and my hope is in You all day long. I praise You, Lord, for You are my shield, my glory, and the One who lifts my head. Keep me as the apple of Your eye, oh God, and hide me under the shadow of Your wings. Even when answers to the injustices I see don't come, I will trust You, for You are truly the only answer I need. In Jesus' name I pray. Amen.

Psalm 91:9; Psalm 46:2–3; Psalm 32:7–8; Psalm 25:5;
Psalm 3:3; Psalm 17:8

My Worship

Your plans are perfect,
Your ways are true.
The depth of Your love is all I need
To carry me through.

Through the storm
I lift my hands to You.
There is no one else who can carry me like You do.
Through the storm
I praise Your name and say,
"Lord, please help me find the way.
I feel all alone but know
You are there to carry me through the storm."

Your grace is sufficient,
Your mercies are new.
The depth of Your love calms my fears
And carries me through.[23]

Reflection and Realignment

Perhaps a particular dilemma has you baffled or dismayed. Come away from the storm to God, your refuge, and settle your mind on His extravagant love. It is unfailing, unconditional, and not minimized or compromised by your need. Ask God to give you His perspective on your circumstances and help you rest in the haven of His care during this storm-tossed time. Commit to praying regularly about this matter until you gain God's peace regarding it.

DAY 24

I AM
Your Redeemer

You are struggling to be still as you feel pressured to make decisions regarding your family's care. Your anxiety threatens your joy, and your efforts to fix things hinder your ability to flow with My Spirit. Cease your striving, and pursue Me. My presence is greater than your greatest struggle, and My power is unlimited. For I am your Redeemer, the Holy One of Israel. I purchased you from the grip of sin, and I want to do a new thing in your life. I want you to walk not in consternation but in the fullness of life that I offer you.

But you must invite Me into your situation. I am completely aware of your trials, but I am waiting for you to call to Me for help. When you do, I will answer. It is time for you to start seeing your trials through My eyes and seeking My presence and power to resolve the dilemmas you face. So many have discarded Me, trusting in their own abilities, but I am the only source of wisdom and strength.

You are trying to make sense of your uncertainties and figure out all the answers. This is not My way for you. My desire for you is to trust Me. I will do for you what you cannot do for yourself. Look beyond the obvious with faith-filled eyes to see My presence in every predicament. I promise to unfold the path before you in My perfect way, and I will keep you from falling.

Look to Me, your Redeemer. I hold the world, the heavens, and your very life in the palm of My hand. I sent My one and only Son, Jesus Christ, to die on the cross to pay the price for your sin so that you wouldn't have to. He is the manifestation of My pure and perfect love. He is the embodiment of My grace. Because of His sacrifice on the cross to redeem you from your sin, you can lay down your anxiety and relax in My finished work. Nothing is impossible for Me.

I have done for you more than you can fully understand. Yet My work is not finished; it is just beginning as you fully surrender each area of your heart and life to Me. I am your greatest ally and your all in all! No matter what pressure you feel, "I have redeemed you; I have called you by your name; you are Mine."

Isaiah 43:14, 19; Titus 2:13–14; Psalm 91:15; Proverbs 3:5; Jude 1:24; Isaiah 44:24; John 3:16; Matthew 19:26; Ephesians 3:20; Isaiah 43:1

God's Promises

Fear not, for I have redeemed you; I have called you by your name; you are Mine. . . . Do not remember the former things, nor consider the things of old. Behold, I will do a new thing, now it shall spring forth; shall you not know it? I will even make a road in the wilderness and rivers in the desert. (Isa. 43:1, 18–19)

Our great God and Savior Jesus Christ . . . gave Himself for us, that He might redeem us from every lawless deed and purify for Himself His own special people, zealous for good works. (Titus 2:13–14)

I have blotted out, like a thick cloud, your transgressions, and like a cloud, your sins. Return to Me, for I have redeemed you. (Isa. 44:22)

With men this is impossible, but with God all things are possible. (Matt. 19:26)

To Him who is able to keep you from stumbling, and to present you faultless before the presence of His glory with exceeding joy, to God our Savior, who alone is wise, be glory and majesty, dominion and power, both now and forever. Amen. (Jude 1:24–25)

My Prayer

Heavenly Father, my God and my Redeemer, I pause now to reflect on Your faithfulness and the splendor of Your majesty. Please forgive me for losing sight of what You have done for me and what You are capable of doing. You have purchased me, and I am Yours. I cannot resolve my struggles, but You can. Help me remember that with You all things are possible. I invite You into my difficulty and in faith believe that You will work it out for my good. Help me, Lord, to trust You fully and walk in the confidence You provide. Help me learn the lessons You want me to learn through my struggles and see Your presence in each and every one. You go before me, and in Your perfect timing and Your perfect way, You will make my crooked paths straight. In faith I receive the treasures You have for me. I will no longer allow myself to be consumed by pressures but will rejoice in the darkness, for even the darkest of nights cannot dispel Your presence or dissolve Your great love. In Jesus' name I pray. Amen.

> Matthew 19:26; Romans 8:28; Isaiah 45:2

My Worship

Teach me Thy way, O Lord, teach me Thy way!
Thy guiding grace afford; teach me Thy way!
Help me to walk aright, more by faith, less by sight;
Lead me with heavenly light; teach me Thy way!

When I am sad at heart, teach me Thy way!
When earthly joys depart, teach me Thy way!
In hours of loneliness, in times of dire distress,
In failure or success, teach me Thy way!

When doubts and fears arise, teach me Thy way!
When storms o'erspread the skies, teach me Thy way!
Shine through the cloud and rain, through sorrow, toil and pain;
Make Thou my pathway plain; teach me Thy way!

Long as my life shall last, teach me Thy way!
Where'er my lot be cast, teach me Thy way!
Until the race is run, until the journey's done,
Until the crown is won, teach me Thy way![24]

Reflection and Realignment

What pressures are you facing? Pause right now and prepare your heart to receive whatever God wants to teach you through this time. Choose one promise from today's devotional reading to apply to your need, and ask God to give you faith that He will meet you in your need. He is your Redeemer; He has purchased you and can make all things new. Nothing is impossible for God!

DAY 25

I AM
Your Sun and Shield

Do not get caught in the trap of people pleasing. The fear of man brings a snare, but whoever trusts in Me will be kept safe. For I, the Lord God, am your sun and shield; I will give grace and glory; no good thing will I withhold from those who walk uprightly. As your sun, I will direct you. As your shield, I will protect you. I will not keep back from you one good thing. Determine now to receive your affirmation from Me and Me alone.

People pleasing will hinder your progress toward healing and distract you from My purpose and plan for your future. Putting too much emphasis on what others think about you will keep you from living abundantly. Break away from the fetter of fearing what others think. People pleasing is a dead-end street; it leads nowhere and leaves you lacking. In contrast, pleasing Me will make you shine. Even your enemies will be at peace with you.

Those people closest to you will at times be disappointed in you, despite your best efforts. That is okay. It is not your job to please or appease them. Just delight in Me, and I will give you the desires of your heart. I created you to glorify Me. People change—their feelings change. They are volatile and vacillate easily. But I never will. My character and affections for you will never vary.

This is why it is so important that you discern My voice above all others and walk daily in My love. My voice speaks peace to your soul, as I accept you just the way you are. You can stop striving for perfection, for I take great delight in you, no matter how well you perform. While people pleasing leads to exhaustion, pleasing Me leads to abundant living. When you decide to obey Me rather than please those around you, you will be set free to be all I have created you to be.

This will not come naturally for you. You have to develop a God-pleasing mentality over a people-pleasing bent by transforming your thinking. Be confident—the work I have started in you will be completed, and My purposes for you will prevail. Stop trusting in your own strength; trust Me instead. Grace and glory are within My grip, and so are you, precious one. Seek to please Me above all others, and you will be amazed at what I will do!

Proverbs 29:25; Psalm 84:11; Proverbs 16:7; Psalm 37:4; Malachi 3:6; Romans 12:2; Philippians 1:6; Proverbs 19:21

God's Promises

The Lord God is a sun and shield; the Lord will give grace and glory; no good thing will He withhold from those who walk uprightly. (Ps. 84:11)

It is better to trust in the Lord than to put confidence in man. (Ps. 118:8)

The fear of man brings a snare, but whoever trusts in the Lord shall be safe. (Prov. 29:25)

Seek first the kingdom of God and His righteousness, and all these things shall be added to you. (Matt. 6:33)

My Prayer

Heavenly Father, thank You that You are my sun and shield. You shine Your light on my way and keep me safe in Your loving care. You are my rock, my deliverer, my strength, and my stronghold. Because You are at my right hand, I will not be shaken. Your presence is the refuge I seek and the safety net that protects me from the advances of my enemies. Exchange my fears for more faith, and give me the wisdom and discernment to resist the temptation to please people. Help me please You and You alone! Thank You for lavishing Your love upon me and for fully accepting me just the way I am. I don't need to perform for You or be perfect. In the stillness of Your presence, I find peace. In the haven of Your heart, I find hope. You, oh Lord, know all about me and love me just the same. My identity is grounded in You, and in Your love my potential is limitless and liberated from the confines of people pleasing. May the words of my mouth and the meditations of my heart be pleasing to You and You alone. In Jesus' name I pray. Amen.

Psalm 18:1–2; Psalm 16:8; Psalm 138:7; Psalm 19:14

My Worship

Day by day, and with each passing moment,
Strength I find to meet my trials here.
Trusting in my Father's wise bestowment,
I've no cause for worry or for fear.
He whose heart is kind beyond all measure
Gives unto each day what He deems best,
Lovingly its part of pain and pleasure,
Mingling toil with peace and rest.

Every day the Lord Himself is near me,
With a special mercy for each hour.
All my cares He fain would bear and cheer me,
He whose name is Counselor and Pow'r.
The protection of His child and treasure
Is a charge that on Himself He laid.
"As thy days, thy strength shall be in measure,"
This the pledge to me He made.

Help me then, in every tribulation,
So to trust Thy promises, O Lord,
That I lose not faith's sweet consolation
Offered me within Thy holy Word.
Help me, Lord, when toil and trouble meeting,
E'er to take, as from a Father's hand,
One by one, the days, the moments fleeting,
Till I reach the promised land.[25]

Reflection and Realignment

Our motives for doing something reveal whether our hearts desire to please the Lord or to please people. Ask the Lord to reveal the motives behind your actions and areas of service—are they to please God or to please man? Write out a prayer, either asking God to help you keep pleasing only Him or recommitting to wholeheartedly serving God and Him alone. Meditate on Colossians 3:23–24.

DAY 26

I AM
Your Confidence

I know you feel forgotten. This is not an easy time for you, especially when you see those around you fast-tracking through their lives without delay. But know that My purpose in removing you from the action was not to punish you but to prepare you for something greater. This should bring you great assurance. I am your confidence, and I will truly bring to completion all I have started in your life. I will make you as surefooted as a deer, and you will stand on the highest heights.

I see you, and I hear your cries for help. I am with you, for "I will never leave you nor forsake you." I have sidelined you but only for a season. I have a purpose in allowing you to experience this time apart.

You see, depth of character is developed through solitude and silence. By putting you on the sideline, I am teaching you to fully trust Me. This temporary exclusion is an opportunity for growth. This preparation is also necessary for the next phase of your life's journey. A new beginning awaits you, but only in My perfect timing will it be revealed. When that time comes, I will discharge you from the bench.

In the meantime, do not compare yourself to others who seem to have it all together. Their success is an illusion, as no one truly has it all together. Also, do not take matters into your own hands by trying to rush this season of waiting. Relax in this time as you "rejoice always, pray without ceasing, in everything give thanks."

Since I am your confidence, I will keep your foot from getting caught in the quicksand of doubt and discouragement, and I will complete the work I'm doing in you. Through you I will raise up the foundations of many generations and repair those areas breached and broken. Stand strong, and do not be discouraged. A new beginning is about to burst forth, and in My perfect timing it will be revealed.

As you wait, cast all your doubt aside, and surrender to My perfect plan. Trust Me, My child, for I am always up to something good even when it does not feel like it to you. Nothing is too difficult for Me to handle or too complicated for Me to fix. "I know the thoughts that I think toward you, . . . thoughts of peace and not of evil, to give you a future and a hope. Then you will call upon Me and go and pray to Me, and I will listen to you. And you will seek Me and find Me, when you search for Me with all your heart."

Proverbs 3:26; Philippians 1:6; Psalm 18:33; Hebrews 13:5;
1 Thessalonians 5:16–18; Isaiah 58:12; Isaiah 41:10;
Isaiah 43:19; Jeremiah 29:11–13

God's Promises

The Lord will be your confidence, and will keep your foot from being caught. (Prov. 3:26)

I Am Your Confidence

Fear not, for I am with you; be not dismayed, for I am your God. I will strengthen you, yes, I will help you, I will uphold you with My righteous right hand. (Isa. 41:10)

[I am] confident of this very thing, that He who has begun a good work in you will complete it until the day of Jesus Christ. (Phil. 1:6)

My Prayer

Heavenly Father, thank You for not only giving me confidence but for *being* my confidence. I am secure in You. Achievements will fade, friends will fall away, and family may not always be there. But You, oh God, will always be present, and in You I can put my trust. Help me embrace this season of waiting and learn the lessons You want me to learn. Though I feel as if I am experiencing a setback, help me be mindful of the progress You are making in me. You are in the process of preparing me for what lies ahead and developing my character to match that call. Your plans for me are perfect, and in Your timing a new beginning will burst forth. Until it does, help me be patient with the process and persevere through this season of delay. Help me not fear or falter out of frustration. I want to keep my eyes firmly fixed upon You. In You, oh Lord, my soul rejoices, for I am not alone. You are always with me, and You empower me to do all things through Christ who gives me strength. Thank You for the quiet assurance and confidence I have in You. I wait on You in hopeful expectation of what is to come. In Jesus' name I pray. Amen.

Matthew 28:20; Psalm 56:4; Psalm 18:30; Isaiah 43:19; Isaiah 41:10; Philippians 4:13

My Worship

Falter not nor look behind thee,
Cast thy every weight aside;
Haste to win the prize before thee,
Trusting Him, thy precious guide.

Falter not nor look behind thee,
Still thy course with joy pursue;
Persevere, for thou must conquer
With the cross of Christ in view.

Falter not nor look behind thee,
Firm and fearless take thy place;
Robe and crown and palm are waiting
For the victors in the race.

Falter not nor look behind thee,
Lest thy labor prove in vain;
Run with patience, and remember
Thou hast much to lose or gain.

Falter not nor look behind thee,
Lo, the prize is just in sight;
One more struggle, meet it bravely,
Speed thee on with all thy might.

Falter not nor look behind thee,
What of all thy trials past,
If by grace through faith in Jesus,
Thine the victor's crown at last?[26]

Reflection and Realignment

What season of adversity are you experiencing as you wait for God to work? Ask God to be your confidence through this time of struggle and to reveal to you the lessons He wants you to learn. Write Philippians 1:6 on a piece of paper, and post it where you can see it often: "He who has begun a good work in you will complete it until the day of Jesus Christ."

DAY 27

I AM
Your Dwelling Place

Your faith is wavering as worry consumes your soul. You are frozen in fear as you try to figure out the dilemma of your family's intensifying needs. Your uncertainty and fear assail you like a storm. But I did not allow these challenges to come into your life for you to struggle through them alone. No, I have allowed these tests to teach you to daily depend upon Me. For I, your eternal God, am your dwelling place, your *Ma'on*, and underneath you are My strong, supportive arms. You are safe and secure in the shelter of My love, and no one can ever remove you from My grip. Do not let another day pass without casting your cares upon My shoulders.

Think about the house you live in. It provides you shelter from the storm, keeping the winds and wild elements out so you can rest peacefully and be protected. In the same way, My presence provides a spiritual shelter from the worries of this world. As you surrender to My leading and allow Me to carry your load, you will find rest—rest for your weary soul. For I, the Lord, am your dwelling place, your refuge, your protection and security from the storm. I have been a dwelling place to My people through all generations, and I am now with you. I am fully present to provide you with peace and strength for the journey ahead. Through the window of My Word you can view your obstacles as opportunities and your challenges as channels of blessing.

Do not be like Peter, who, when walking on the water, began to sink because he shifted his focus from Me. Keep your eyes fixed on Me. Call to Me, and I will answer you. Come to Me, and I will care for you like no other. As you look to Me, I will keep your soul from sinking as I settle you with My all-sufficient grace. My strength is plentiful and perfect. In your weakness I am strong, and all My promises are yes and amen.

Though the darkness seems to consume you, it is only temporary, for soon the sun will shine, and the difficulties of your day will depart as I, your eternal God, make all things new.

Psalm 91:9–10; Deuteronomy 33:27; John 10:28; 1 Peter 5:7; Matthew 11:29; Psalm 90:1–2; Matthew 14:29–30; Jeremiah 33:3; Psalm 103:13–14; 2 Corinthians 12:9; 2 Corinthians 1:20; Revelation 21:5

God's Promises

Lord, You have been our dwelling place in all generations. Before the mountains were brought forth, or ever You had formed the earth and the world, even from everlasting to everlasting, You are God. (Ps. 90:1–2)

Because you have made the LORD, who is my refuge, even the Most High, your dwelling place, no evil shall befall you, nor shall any plague come near your dwelling. (Ps. 91:9–10)

How lovely is Your tabernacle, O LORD of hosts! My soul longs, yes, even faints for the courts of the LORD; my heart and my flesh cry out for the living God. (Ps. 84:1–2)

My tabernacle also shall be with them; indeed I will be their God, and they shall be My people. (Ezek. 37:27)

My Prayer

Heavenly Father, thank You for being my dwelling place. Help me rest in the safety of Your shelter, Lord. Many are my cares and concerns, but I cast them all upon You. Forgive me, oh God, for getting so overwhelmed by the storms of my life that I forget You and Your prevailing presence and protection over me. Father, help me trust You with everything I am going through and see it all through Your eyes. Help me lean not on my own understanding and acknowledge You in all my ways. You are in control, and only You can turn my troubles into triumphs. I will fully depend upon You as I rest in Your presence and take shelter in the dwelling place of Your eternal love. In Jesus' name I pray. Amen.

1 Peter 5:7; Proverbs 3:5–6

My Worship

I know my heavenly Father knows
The storms that would my way oppose;
But He can drive the clouds away
And turn the darkness into day.

He knows, He knows
The storms that would my way oppose;
He knows, He knows
And tempers every wind that blows.

I know my heavenly Father knows
The balm I need to soothe my woes;
And with His touch of love divine
He heals this wounded heart of mine.

I know my heavenly Father knows
How frail I am to meet my foes;
But He my cause will e'er defend,
Uphold and keep me to the end.

I know my heavenly Father knows
The hour my journey here will close;
And may that hour, O faithful Guide,
Find me safe sheltered by Thy side.[27]

Reflection and Realignment

Consider whether you are dwelling under the shelter of God's care or out in the storm of your many worries and concerns. Take some time to praise God for being your dwelling place, and ask Him to help you rest under His protection. He is your place of peace, your haven of hope, your shelter through the storm.

DAY 28

I AM
Your Hope

Dear child, many are the pressures surrounding you, but the greatest pressures are those within you. You try to set boundaries and create balance in order to protect your heart from the expectations of others, but nevertheless you find yourself back at square one, hurt and poisoned by unkind words. You are weary and worn, tired of spinning your wheels and getting nowhere. Your wavering emotions and feelings of uncertainty make you feel like giving up. In this quiet season of deep reflection, I am your hope, and you can fully trust in Me. My provisions are limitless and always available to meet your every need. Your struggles are My struggles. Your concerns are My concerns. Release your unrest, and find solace for your soul in My presence.

My desire for you is hopeful expectation. As you entrust your cares to Me, I will carry your load and give you exactly what you need to walk through this day. Come to Me with absolute dependence, like a baby bird that is desperately dependent upon its mother for its next bite of food. You too must be desperately dependent upon Me. Apart from Me you can do nothing, but with Me you can do all things. I can exchange your fear for more faith, your insecurity for My stability, and your discouragement for hope.

As your God, I am your covenant partner. My obligation to you is to keep My promises. Whatever your difficulty, My provision is more than enough. When negative thoughts nag you, use them as a catalyst to draw near to Me. Negate those thoughts with My promises. Allow absolute expectancy to drive your thoughts and feelings toward hope. My hope does not disappoint.

As your God of hope, I will "fill you with all joy and peace in believing, that you may abound in hope by the power of the Holy Spirit." I brought My people, the Israelites, out of bondage, and I will set you free as well. This spacious place is called "grace." Receive it, and allow it to revive you. Open your mouth wide, and I will fill it. See what great things I can do!

Psalm 33:20–22; Philippians 4:19; 2 Peter 1:3; John 15:5; Philippians 4:13; Romans 5:5; Romans 15:13; Psalm 81:10

God's Promises

Blessed be the God and Father of our Lord Jesus Christ, who according to His abundant mercy has begotten us again to a living hope through the resurrection of Jesus Christ from the dead. (1 Pet. 1:3)

Why are you cast down, O my soul? And why are you disquieted within me? Hope in God; for I shall yet praise Him, the help of my countenance and my God. (Ps. 42:11)

Happy is he who has the God of Jacob for his help, whose hope is in the Lord his God. (Ps. 146:5)

Whatever things were written before were written for our learning, that we through the patience and comfort of the Scriptures might have hope. (Rom. 15:4)

Hope does not disappoint, because the love of God has been poured out in our hearts by the Holy Spirit who was given to us. (Rom. 5:5)

My Prayer

Heavenly Father, thank You for being my hope. In the midst of this time of uncertainty, when temptations loom within my soul, I look to You, the divine author of hope. As my faith falters and my feelings waver, I seek to settle my heart on You and the hope You provide. Like a flowing stream that gives life to the sun-parched land around it, I ask You to resurrect hope in my heart. Help me not give up but rather to stand strong in the hope You provide. I trust You to sustain me through this desert-like time. As I open my mouth, You will fill it. Nothing is impossible for You, oh God, or beyond Your infinite reach. With You I have victory. Thank You for being my hope. In Jesus' name I pray. Amen.

Psalm 81:10; Matthew 19:26; 1 Corinthians 15:57

My Worship

My hope is built on nothing less
Than Jesus' blood and righteousness;

I dare not trust the sweetest frame
But wholly lean on Jesus' name.

On Christ, the solid Rock, I stand;
All other ground is sinking sand,
All other ground is sinking sand.

When darkness veils His lovely face,
I rest on His unchanging grace;
In every high and stormy gale,
My anchor holds within the veil.

His oath, His covenant, His blood
Support me in the whelming flood;
When all around my soul gives way,
He then is all my hope and stay.

When He shall come with trumpet sound,
Oh, may I then in Him be found;
Dressed in His righteousness alone,
Faultless to stand before the throne.[28]

Reflection and Realignment

The deepest level of worship is praising God when we are at our lowest. Take some time to listen to some uplifting praise music or sing to the Lord in the midst of your difficulties. In spite of the trials you may be encountering, praise God for being your hope.

DAY 29

I AM
Your Portion

You are walking in discouragement because of the lies you believe. The enemy has prompted you to use negative self-talk in order to stunt your growth and hinder your progress. This has given you a flawed perspective. You have spent your life comparing yourself to others while using what seem to be their perfect performances as your guide. This leads only to lingering feelings of inadequacy. I, however, desire to fill the empty places of your soul with all that I am and fill you to overflowing. I am your portion, which means that I give and keep on giving of Myself to make you all I want you to be. I fill the empty places of your soul completely. No need to look elsewhere—I am near, and I have qualified you to do good works.

Learn to recognize the negative voices. So subtle are their murmurs that unless you seek Me for discernment, you can quickly become caught in a downward spiral. As you step back to consider your thoughts and what they are conveying to your soul, you will be able to discern whether those thoughts are true or false.

As long as you compare yourself to others, your growth will be hindered. The seeming perfection you see in others is an illusion; people will always appear more capable and equipped on the outside than they truly are. But what I am doing on the inside of a person is a far greater work than what people see on the outside. This is what you are missing. As you lie here inactive, I am building in you character that is far better than any seemingly perfect performance. I have branded you as beautiful, inside and out. I, the One who sees and knows your potential, provide you with a portion of all I am to equip you to fulfill My special purposes. As you grow in grace as My image bearer, you will shine like a star in the universe. Trust Me. Your destiny is in My hands.

Do not allow the voices of naysayers and your own negative self-talk to deter you from wholeheartedly believing Me. Though your flesh and heart may fail, I am the strength of your heart and your portion forever. When you receive people's criticism, stay centered on My promises, for My thoughts are the only ones that truly matter. When I see you, I see My child, precious and dearly loved, blameless and empowered as My ambassador. The trials of this world may get you down, but I am more than enough to lift you up.

Allow My unfailing love to saturate your entire being and transform you into the person I made you to be. No matter what others say, you are the work of My hands. You are a gem in the making. You are being shaped for My special purposes. Wait upon Me, for I am your portion. Surrender, and I will completely satisfy you. It is time for you to stop spinning your wheels. The hour has come for you to just *breathe*.

Lamentations 3:24; James 4:8; Ephesians 2:10;
Philippians 2:15; Psalm 73:26; Psalm 16:5

God's Promises

"The LORD is my portion," says my soul, "therefore I hope in Him!" (Lam. 3:24)

I cried out to You, O LORD: I said, "You are my refuge, my portion in the land of the living." (Ps. 142:5)

Blessed be the LORD, because He has heard the voice of my supplications! The LORD is my strength and my shield; my heart trusted in Him, and I am helped; therefore my heart greatly rejoices, and with my song I will praise Him. (Ps. 28:6–7)

My flesh and my heart fail; but God is the strength of my heart and my portion forever. (Ps. 73:26)

My Prayer

Heavenly Father, thank You for being my portion. In You I find hope. Oh, how great is Your goodness that You call me Your child and prepare me for Your purposes. Though I feel inept and lacking, You, oh God, have qualified me. You are the only measuring stick I need. Please forgive me for comparing myself to others and listening to the negative voices inside my mind. You have the power to do so much more in me than I could ever imagine. Strengthen my faith, and help me receive Your promises at the core of my being. I am tired of striving, spinning my wheels and getting nowhere. I surrender to You all I am and all I have. Exchange my feelings of defeat, oh God, for victory—the victory I have in You. Lord, in You I am more than a conqueror, and I have everything I need to live this life well. Help me to believe this in the depths of my heart. Thank You for enlightening my darkness with the light of Your unfailing love. It is You who arms me with strength and makes my way perfect. Blessed be Your holy name. In Jesus' name I pray. Amen.

Romans 8:37; 2 Peter 1:3; Psalm 18:32

My Worship

In heavenly love abiding, no change my heart shall fear;
And safe is such confiding, for nothing changes here.
The storm may roar without me, my heart may low be laid,
But God is round about me, and can I be dismayed?

Wherever He may guide me, no want shall turn me back;
My shepherd is beside me, and nothing can I lack.
His wisdom ever taketh; His sight is never dim.
He knows the way He taketh, and I will walk with Him.

Green pastures are before me which yet I have not seen.
Bright skies will soon be o'er me, where darkest clouds have been.
My hope I cannot measure; my path to life is free.
My Savior has my treasure, and He will walk with me.[29]

Reflection and Realignment

Sit still in God's presence as you meditate on Lamentations 3:24. Allow your thoughts to linger on who God is and the peace, contentment, and joy He provides. Now write out a prayer asking Him to be your portion—to fill the empty places of your soul with all that He is. When God gives, He gives to overflowing. He is more than enough.

DAY 30

I AM
Your Song

Why are you dismayed? Feelings of disappointment drive you into a pit of despair. You feel crushed because the people closest to you have misunderstood your inner needs during this season and let you down. Though it is your natural tendency to look to them for affirmation, this will only lead to emptiness. Even the most reliable people will at some time disappoint you. Not so with Me. I am your song. I will lift your countenance and fill your heart with cheer. The discouragement you are facing now will not remain as you keep your thoughts fixed on Me.

I love you, My child, and My love for you will never fail. Learn to view My love as your affirming power. Nothing will impede your progress when you see My love as your source of joy and strength. Without realizing it, you have elevated people in your heart. This is your blind spot. See this for what it is, and release these individuals from this lofty place. Friends may fail you, family members may fall away or misunderstand you, and people may label you and misrepresent you, but My love for you will never end. In this you can rejoice.

My love is the source of your song. I am constantly thinking of you and seeking your best. With My sights set on you, I woo you toward Me. I want you to experience the depth of My love and joy in your innermost being. My extravagant love is your gift. Like a song that moves you to dance, so My love motivates you to action. Receive it, and let it revive you. Rest in it, and let it redirect you—changing your perspective and producing in you a glad, immovable stance that does not fold to opposition or give in to discouragement. My love for you is eternal—even before you were, it was, and since it is not dependent upon you, it always will be. Embrace it today, and allow it to embrace you. I love you on your good days and on your bad ones. I love you when your attitude needs adjusting and when you radiate joy. I love you even when you choose not to love Me.

You will gain strength as I turn your pain into songs of praise. Your victory is in My hands. Celebrate the small steps! I'm in the process of doing a new thing. Just as I was with the psalmist David, so I am with you. While he patiently persevered through his season of waiting, I pursued him: I did not forget him or abandon him but instead provided for him a firm place to stand and put a new song in his mouth. I will do the same for you.

As the anthem of My love drowns out the old dirges of discouragement within your soul, your hope and gladness will revive, and your healing will begin. Nothing can ever separate you from My love. Rest in it today, and receive it as your own.

Exodus 15:2; Isaiah 26:3; 1 Corinthians 13:8; Psalm 136:1; Philippians 4:7; Isaiah 43:19; Psalm 40:1–3; Romans 8:39

God's Promises

It is better to trust in the LORD than to put confidence in man. . . . The LORD is my strength and song, and He has become my salvation. (Ps. 118:8, 14)

I waited patiently for the LORD; and He inclined to me, and heard my cry. He also brought me up out of a horrible pit, out of the miry clay, and set my feet upon a rock, and established my steps. He has put a new song in my mouth—praise to our God; many will see it and fear, and will trust in the LORD. (Ps. 40:1–3)

The LORD will command His lovingkindness in the daytime, and in the night His song shall be with me—a prayer to the God of my life. (Ps. 42:8)

You shall have a song as in the night when a holy festival is kept, and gladness of heart as when one goes with a flute, to come into the mountain of the LORD, to the Mighty One of Israel. (Isa. 30:29)

My Prayer

Heavenly Father, thank You for being my song and for giving my heart a new melody. Your love deeply satisfies my soul and brings me hope. Forgive me for putting confidence in man more than in You. Though I have encountered several disappointments, You, oh God, are always with me and promise to go before me. Your love for me is constant and will never end. Thank You for being fully trustworthy. I trust You with those areas of my life that I find most difficult. I trust You to have my best interests in mind and to provide the best outcome to my situations. As I wait upon You for the fulfillment of Your plan for me, help me be more like You—to see those around me with Your eyes, love those around me with Your heart, and feel for those around me with Your compassion. I want to be fully alive in You, not held back by past hurts and heartaches but renewed and refreshed by Your presence. Fulfill Your promise to restore to me the joy of Your salvation and uphold me by Your Holy Spirit. In Jesus' name I pray. Amen.

Deuteronomy 31:8; 1 Corinthians 13:8; Psalm 51:12

My Worship

Open my eyes that I may see
All the wonders You have for me.
Open my heart that I may know
Every place You want me to go.

I am Yours, Lord;
Take my hand.
Lead me, guide me, through this land.
I am Yours, Lord;
Fill me today
With Your love so amazing.
I want to give it away.

Be my vision, my hope, my all;
Carry me through
So I may not fall.
Protect me from the enemy's plan;
Hold me safely in Your hand.

> Fill my heart afresh, anew;
> Give me eyes to see Your truth.
> Enfold me in Your love divine
> Until I am no longer mine.[30]

Reflection and Realignment

Savor a moment of resting in God's strength. He is your song and desires to put a spring in your step. Though things may seem grim, God is still in control. All outcomes are in His hands, and nothing is impossible for Him. Meditate on Psalm 40:1–3, and write out your own song of praise to God for His goodness—even if you can't see the good in your circumstances yet.

DAY 31

I AM YOUR DELIVERER

In this life you will encounter many distresses and difficulties. Seasons of adversity will come. But even when everything around you seems to be spinning out of control, I, your deliverer, will see you through. I know you are worried about your children's hearts during this season when you are unwell, but I am with you and your family, and I am for each one of you. You can remain confident in Me. You do not need to fear, for My presence is sure, and My protection is certain. Because you love Me, I will rescue you. Because you acknowledge My name, I will set you on high. When you call to Me, I will answer, and I will deliver you as I walk with you through your troubling time.

It is natural for you to desire seasons in your life when all is well. No one wants to encounter adversity. But only through times of testing will you come to experience My love most deeply. As your deliverer, I will surround you with songs of liberation. Your freedom has come! You don't need to feel powerless in the face of opposition, for I am your power source through all your problems. Stay connected to Me, and watch how I will give you exactly what you need. Even the most challenging tests can be doorways to experience My presence more deeply. Your afflictions may be many, but I will see you through.

Do not fear tomorrow, dear child, for I hold tomorrow in My hand. Every obstacle ahead of you is already within My grip. Nothing is a mystery to Me, and nothing is a mistake. Every problem is an opportunity for Me to manifest more of Myself to you, and every case you encounter is an opportunity for you to grow. I was with Shadrach, Meshach, and Abednego through the fiery furnace, and I will be with you. I delivered them from the cruel hand of King Nebuchadnezzar, and I will deliver you too.

No hand is greater than Mine, and no god is greater than Me. The sooner you can view your time of testing through My eyes, the stronger you will become. I allow times of testing in your life not to harm or hurt you but to show you those areas of your heart that are not yet fully yielded to Me.

Your negative emotions in the midst of distress are a caution light reminding you to reexamine your thoughts. The mind is powerful. Pleasant emotions flow from peaceful thoughts, and painful emotions flow from painful thoughts. Although I have designed you to experience emotion, I desire for you to harness your emotions in positive ways by giving them over to Me. Reacting to your fears and concerns will only cause damage, but responding to them will release you to be still and know that I am God. Cast your many cares upon Me.

John 16:33; Psalm 18:2; Isaiah 41:10; Romans 8:31; Psalm 91:14–15; Psalm 32:7; Psalm 34:19; Daniel 3:19–30; Psalm 46:10; 1 Peter 5:7

God's Promises

The Lord is my rock and my fortress and my deliverer; my God, my strength, in whom I will trust; my shield and the horn of my salvation, my stronghold. (Ps. 18:2)

I am poor and needy; yet the LORD thinks upon me. You are my help and my deliverer; do not delay, O my God. (Ps. 40:17)

Fear not, for I am with you; be not dismayed, for I am your God. I will strengthen you, yes, I will help you, I will uphold you with My righteous right hand. (Isa. 41:10)

What then shall we say to these things? If God is for us, who can be against us? (Rom. 8:31)

Because he has set his love upon Me, therefore I will deliver him; I will set him on high, because he has known My name. He shall call upon Me, and I will answer him; I will be with him in trouble; I will deliver him and honor him. With long life I will satisfy him, and show him My salvation. (Ps. 91:14–16)

My Prayer

Heavenly Father, thank You for promising to be my deliverer. I admit that I have been anxious. The distresses I am facing have me tied up in knots. Help me, Lord, to refocus my attention on You—to be still and know that You are God, You are in control, and You have good plans for me, despite what I see. As I take this moment to still myself in Your presence, I hand all my cares over to You and exchange my anxiety-filled thoughts for Your thoughts of love and peace. I know You love me, Lord, and have my best interests in mind even though I do not feel it at the moment. I say to my storm-tossed soul, "I trust You, God." I trust You for this moment. I trust You for this day. And I trust You for tomorrow. I stand upon that which is true, noble, just, pure, lovely, and good and to walk forward, one small step at a time, in trusting obedience to You. In Jesus' name I pray. Amen.

Psalm 46:10; Jeremiah 29:11; Philippians 4:6–9

My Worship

O hear my cry, be gracious now to me,
Come, great deliverer, come;
My soul bowed down is longing now for Thee,
Come, great deliverer, come.

I've wandered far away o'er mountains cold,
I've wandered far away from home;
O take me now, and bring me to Thy fold,
Come, great deliverer, come.

I have no place, no shelter from the night,
Come, great deliverer, come;
One look from Thee would give me life and light,
Come, great deliverer, come.

My path is lone, and weary are my feet,
Come, great deliverer, come;
Mine eyes look up Thy loving smile to meet,
Come, great deliverer, come.

> Thou wilt not spurn contrition's broken sigh,
> Come, great deliverer, come.
> Regard my prayer, and hear my humble cry,
> Come, great deliverer, come.[31]

Reflection and Realignment

What dilemma do you need deliverance from? Sometimes God chooses to deliver us *from* our problems, and other times He chooses to deliver us *in* our problems by giving us the grace and strength to walk through them with Him by our side. Read Isaiah 41:10, and commit to memorizing it over the next week. Then ask the Lord to be your deliverer, and wait to see what He will do.

DAY 32

I AM
THE GOD WHO HEARS YOU

It is so easy for you to travel through life depending on your own resources and means. But I have created you to be different—to be fully dependent upon Me. And you *can* depend on Me, because I am the God who hears you when you call. Many do not have their needs met because they simply neglect to ask for My help. While I do not promise to provide all you want, I do promise to provide all you need. The more you trust Me to hear your cries, the more you will experience My care for you.

Choose today to pray. I heard Hannah's cry for help, and I hear yours. Through tears and turmoil, Hannah prayed for a son. Deeply troubled, she poured out her soul. Her womb was closed. She felt useless. She felt hopeless. Yet in that place of despair, she did not stop praying. In her pain, she did not neglect to plead. I heard her. I saw her. I remembered her and answered her—and I will answer you.

So come to Me boldly, request confidently, and know that if you ask anything according to My will, I hear you. Though at times My answers may seem vague or not what you expected, My answers are always rendered with your best interests in mind. I alone know how your petitions fit into the scope of My purposes. When you seek Me and I answer no, or I ask you to wait, recognize that these responses are as much out of My love for you as when I answer yes. From your limited viewpoint you only see a portion of your life, but I see it all. Trust Me, My child; I am in the process of working all things together for your good and for My glory.

Jeremiah 29:11–12; James 4:2; Philippians 4:19; 1 Samuel 1:12–20; 1 John 5:14; Proverbs 5:21; Romans 8:28

God's Promises

Know that the LORD has set apart for Himself him who is godly; the LORD will hear when I call to Him. (Ps. 4:3)

This is the confidence that we have in Him, that if we ask anything according to His will, He hears us. And if we know that He hears us, whatever we ask, we know that we have the petitions that we have asked of Him. (1 John 5:14–15)

Certainly God has heard me; He has attended to the voice of my prayer. Blessed be God, who has not turned away my prayer, nor His mercy from me! (Ps. 66:19–20)

Ask, and it will be given to you; seek, and you will find; knock, and it will be opened to you. For everyone who asks receives, and he who seeks finds, and to him who knocks it will be opened. (Matt. 7:7–8)

My Prayer

Heavenly Father, thank You for hearing me. Forgive me for depending on my own resources and not trusting You to hear my prayers. When I call to You, You answer. When I cry out to You, You care. When I pray in faith, believing, You listen, and You are always with me. You are always there. You know my pain before I express it. You know my need before I call. You know my heartache, and You feel it. You help me up after I fall. Thank You for reminding me of Your promise to hear me when I pray. I can come to You confidently with all my troubles and know that You will not turn Your ear away. Please forgive me for the times I have neglected You and ceased to recognize Your hand. By Your grace I will move forward; by Your grace I will stand. You do not neglect my earnest pleas; You receive my heartfelt prayers. Thank You for being a God who hears—and truly cares. In Jesus' name I pray. Amen.

Psalm 17:6; Psalm 18:6; Matthew 21:22; Joshua 1:9;
Psalm 37:24; 1 John 5:14

My Worship

Sweet hour of prayer, sweet hour of prayer,
That calls me from a world of care
And bids me at my Father's throne
Make all my wants and wishes known!
In seasons of distress and grief
My soul has often found relief
And oft escaped the tempter's snare
By thy return, sweet hour of prayer.

Sweet hour of prayer! Sweet hour of prayer!
The joy I feel, the bliss I share
Of those whose anxious spirits burn
With strong desires for thy return!
With such I hasten to the place
Where God my Savior shows His face,
And gladly take my station there
And wait for thee, sweet hour of prayer!

Sweet hour of prayer! Sweet hour of prayer!
Thy wings shall my petition bear
To Him whose truth and faithfulness
Engage the waiting soul to bless;
And since He bids me seek His face,
Believe His Word and trust His grace,
I'll cast on Him my every care
And wait for thee, sweet hour of prayer![32]

Reflection and Realignment

Choose one of God's promises in today's reading, and apply it to a dilemma or difficulty you are currently experiencing. Write out your need, with the promise next to it, and date it. Then wait in hopeful expectation for God to answer. When He does, write down the answer and the date of the answer next to your original need as a testimony to God's faithfulness.

DAY 33

I AM
Your Father of Glory

I am aware that during this time in your life I seem quiet. You may feel that I have rejected you, but I am working behind the scenes of your life, putting pieces into place for the work I have for you to do. I am your loving Father of glory, and I desire to powerfully reveal Myself to you and do more for you than you could ever ask or imagine.

Just as I was with Moses and My people, the Israelites, so am I with you. They experienced My presence in a pillar of cloud and pillar of fire, but you can experience Me and My glory in an even greater way today. Through the guidance of My Spirit, I impart to you the same power that rose My Son, Jesus Christ, from the dead and seated Him in the heavenlies. Do not anxiously look around you, but rather look to Me. For where My Spirit is, there is freedom, and where My Spirit is, there is life.

I desire to reveal more of My glory to you, but that can only happen as you draw near to Me, even though I may seem far away. Through your submission, I set the stage for My glory to be revealed, not in a pillar of cloud or a pillar of fire, but in and through the life of My Son, Jesus Christ. When you see Him, you see Me. In knowing Him, you know Me. His love, forgiveness, mercy, kindness, compassion, and grace are all gifts of My glory—freely given to you to make your heart soar! Receive them now, and rest in Me. You are loved; you are treasured; you are Mine.

Do not allow this time of silence to stir up frustration within you, for I will never leave you or forsake you. I am with you always, even to the end of the age. Trust Me. I have a plan for the silence and a purpose for your pain. Instead of complaining, allow this time to be a catalyst to press into My presence and prepare you for what is to come.

As you encounter My silence, you are still encountering Me. My glory transcends the silence, and the silence draws you into My glory. I have not rejected you; I am simply pruning you and preparing you for what is to come. My silence is not a signal to give up; it is a sign to press forward and persevere in prayer. My silence is more of an answer than you think, because it brings you to a greater awareness of who I am. Be stilled by the silence, and do not allow it to stir up feelings of abandonment. You are being protected in the shadow of My almighty wings.

My silence toward My children is not something new. Godly people have experienced it throughout the ages. Job encountered My silence through his tribulations. Though his suffering was unbearable, he recognized Me in the midst of his trials as the One who can do everything and whose purposes to bring good out of evil will not be thwarted. You too must cling to Me, especially during your times of confusion, when you might perceive My silence as distance and cannot make sense of your chronic pain. During these times, you can be certain of My love for you and My sovereignty over your life. So arise, shine; for your light has come! My glory is risen upon you.

Ephesians 1:17–20; Ephesians 3:20; Exodus 13:21; 2 Corinthians 3:17; John 6:63; James 4:8; Colossians 1:15; Deuteronomy 31:6; Matthew 28:20; Philippians 4:6–7; Psalm 91:4; Job 42:2; Luke 18:1–8; Ephesians 2:4; Psalm 103:19; Isaiah 60:1

God's Promises

Arise, shine; for your light has come! And the glory of the LORD is risen upon you. (Isa. 60:1)

We all, with unveiled face, beholding as in a mirror the glory of the Lord, are being transformed into the same image from glory to glory, just as by the Spirit of the Lord. (2 Cor. 3:18)

[I pray] that the God of our Lord Jesus Christ, the Father of glory, may give to you the spirit of wisdom and revelation in the knowledge of Him, the eyes of your understanding being enlightened; that you may know what is the hope of His calling, what are the riches of the glory of His inheritance in the saints, and what is the exceeding greatness of His power toward us who believe, according to the working of His mighty power which He worked in Christ when He raised Him from the dead. (Eph. 1:17–20)

The LORD went before them by day in a pillar of cloud to lead the way, and by night in a pillar of fire to give them light, so as to go by day and night. (Exod. 13:21)

My Prayer

Father of glory, I come humbly before You and ask You to forgive me for thinking that Your silence means that You do not care. I do know that You care for me and love me, but I am struggling to make sense of my circumstances. Thank You for revealing Your glory to me in Your Son, Jesus Christ, and for not giving up on me. Your love never fails, and Your grace will see me through this tough time. Although it feels as if Your promises are being contradicted by my struggles, I will trust that Your promises are true and that none of Your purposes will be thwarted. You are the Almighty God, and nothing is impossible for You. You give me life and breath, and You can bring good out of the evil around me. Help me, Lord, to see my situation through Your eyes, and enable me by Your Spirit to develop Your perspective amid my troubling times. There is nothing I want more, oh God, than to have Your purposes fulfilled in my life. Help me accept Your ways and see Your glory revealed in my life today. In Jesus' name I pray. Amen.

Psalm 136:1–2; 2 Corinthians 12:9; Job 42:2; Luke 1:37;
Job 33:4; Romans 8:28

My Worship

You reign in majesty;
You lift me up from all my frailties.
You reign in power;
You hold me in Your hand.

We have seen Your glory,
We have seen Your glory, O Lord.
We have seen Your glory,
Your glory from above.

> You reign in righteousness;
> You guide me through this world with Your truth.
> You reign eternally;
> You are the great I AM.[33]

Reflection and Realignment

When have you experienced a season in your life when God seemed silent—when life didn't make sense and you felt as if your prayers were hitting the ceiling? Write about this season, and reflect on how you responded to God's silence. Whether you withdrew from God or remained close to Him, draw near to Him again, sit still in His presence, and thank Him for never leaving you or forsaking you.

DAY 34

I AM
THE MAKER OF ALL THINGS

If I remain silent, it is because I am not ready to reveal the fullness of My purposes to you. The timing isn't right. But I am still working behind the scenes in ways you cannot see. Just because you do not see Me working does not mean I am doing nothing. I am the "God who makes everything," which means that I am the maker and manager of your waiting seasons. I initiate these times as well as ordain their endings.

Often when the reason for My delay is unclear, discouragement sets in, because you somehow relate My silence to separation from Me. Guard your heart, precious child, from this fallacy. Stand strong in Me and in the power of My might. Seek Me with all your heart. Wait upon Me in hopeful expectation. I am present with you in each of your needs, and I have a plan even for My apparent delays.

When you experience these delays, trust Me. Press into My promises. They will keep you grounded during this time of uncertainty. If My direction is not clear, wait. If you do not hear My whisper, wait. If details are not aligning, wait. If you do not know what to do, wait. If you are struggling to find answers, wait. Waiting upon Me is not an arbitrary activity but an active, prayer-filled stance. It requires effort, focus, and fortitude. Waiting involves trusting that I will answer and that, no matter what, I will see you through. I have created the times of waiting you encounter in order to shape your character for the next phase of your journey. Receive this difficult season with gratitude, and refocus your attention away from the wait and onto Me. I am just as much in the waiting as I am in the activity of your life.

Use this season of waiting to get to know Me more. I desire to reveal so much more to you about Me than I have before, but you must remove yourself from the distractions that occupy your time and attention. You hear how others are experiencing Me, but you doubt in your heart that you too can experience this same level of intimacy. In reality, I am at work within you and all around you. I am in the process of making all things new. Can you see it?

Do not be satisfied to merely know about Me; seek to experience Me through the details of your day. Upon waking, the breath you breathe is that which I supply. The food you eat was given to you by My hand. Your home, your clothing, your job, your family, and your existence are all gifts of My goodness. Focus on these gifts with a grateful heart. Let your gentleness be evident to all, for I am near to you.

One of the most difficult things in life is to wait—it does not come easily even to the most mature in its classroom. But if you learn to embrace the waiting seasons I create in your life, you will receive great rewards. As you patiently pursue the lessons I want to teach you, your growth will increase, and your faith muscles will be strengthened. It is only in the waiting seasons that these valuable lessons can be learned most effectively. Before you know it, a new day will dawn, and a new season will arrive. The wait will not last forever, so receive it as a gift. It is My most fruit-bearing blessing.

Ecclesiastes 11:5; Ephesians 6:10; Jeremiah 29:13; Psalm 27:14; Philippians 1:6; John 5:17; Revelation 21:5; Philippians 4:5

God's Promises

By Him all things were created that are in heaven and that are on earth, visible and invisible, whether thrones or dominions or principalities or powers. All things were created through Him and for Him. And He is before all things, and in Him all things consist. (Col. 1:16–17)

To everything there is a season, a time for every purpose under heaven. . . . He has made everything beautiful in its time. (Eccles. 3:1, 11)

In Your book they all were written, the days fashioned for me, when as yet there were none of them. (Ps. 139:16)

A word spoken in due season, how good it is! (Prov. 15:23)

Let us not grow weary while doing good, for in due season we shall reap if we do not lose heart. (Gal. 6:9)

My Prayer

Heavenly Father, thank You for being the maker of all things, even my waiting seasons. But I must confess to You that I am struggling to accept this waiting season as a gift of Your goodness. I am feeling rejected, as if You have benched me and forgotten me on the sidelines. Help me, Lord, to learn the lessons You have for me through this difficult season. Your Word says that a bruised reed You will not break and smoking flax You will not snuff out. I know that I can trust Your promises, Lord, but my faith is faltering as I doubt whether I will ever rise from the sidelines. Lord, strengthen my heart as I wait on You. I stand firm on Your promises and hold fast to Your truth. Since You are the divine maker of all things, I trust that You will end this season of waiting in Your perfect timing. Until then, help me to embrace the wait and keep my focus on You. I receive this waiting season as a blessing, not a burden, for You are always good, oh God, and have my best interests in mind. Thank You, Lord, for revealing Your love and care for me. I choose now to receive this time of waiting according to Your will and surrender my life to Your plan. In Jesus' name I pray. Amen.

Isaiah 42:2; Psalm 27:14

My Worship

When peace, like a river, attendeth my way,
When sorrows like sea billows roll,
Whatever my lot, Thou hast taught me to say,
"It is well, it is well with my soul."

It is well
With my soul.
It is well, it is well with my soul.

Though Satan should buffet, though trials should come,
Let this blest assurance control,
That Christ hath regarded my helpless estate
And hath shed His own blood for my soul.

> My sin—O the bliss of this glorious thought! —
> My sin, not in part, but the whole
> Is nailed to the cross, and I bear it no more!
> Praise the Lord, praise the Lord, O my soul!
>
> And, Lord, haste the day when the faith shall be sight,
> The clouds be rolled back as a scroll,
> The trump shall resound, and the Lord shall descend,
> Even so—it is well with my soul.[34]

Reflection and Realignment

Doubt and discouragement can easily set in during seasons of waiting, and we can feel as if God is nowhere to be found. In such times we are tempted to take matters into our own hands. If you feel this way, remember that God is just as much at work in your waiting season as He is in the times of activity in your life. When things don't seem to be moving fast enough or falling into place, trust God. Choose one of God's promises from today's devotional reading to claim over your waiting season. Read this promise daily over the next week, asking God to grow in you a faith that will believe Him for a beautiful outcome.

DAY 35

I AM
THE LORD YOUR GOD

As you look at the world around you, you see peril. Devastation, destruction, disease, and difficulties obscure your view. Corruption increases, and you feel powerless to make a change. Anxiety creeps into your heart as these wider concerns compound your personal fears. Though your concerns and cares are valid, they are not meant for you to carry. Look to Me, and give Me your load. When life spins out of control and all hope seems lost, look to Me, for I am the Lord your God, your continual source and supply of help.

Do not become embittered by the injustices you see and the trials you face. I, who made heaven and earth, delight in resurrecting life from the ashes of difficulties. View the positive by choosing to see Me in the midst of your pain-filled moments. I am at work all around you, and I sit on My heavenly throne watching over you and My entire creation. No person is hidden from My view, and no evil act will go unpunished. I neither slumber nor sleep, and I scan the whole earth to strongly support those whose hearts are fully committed to Me.

It is time for you to draw near to Me as you never have before. "Incline your ear, and come to Me. Hear, and your soul shall live." Seek Me while I may be found. Call upon Me while I am near.

Taste and see that I am good. Come to Me, the Lord your God, for I am gracious and merciful, slow to anger, and of great kindness. I relent from doing harm. The relationship I offer you is real and readily available. Come to Me with childlike faith, and watch what I can do.

By adjusting your life to Me and surrendering to My lordship, you will experience a new level of My presence and power. Corruption and peril in the world, past pain in your personal life, worries about your future—none of these need make you fearful. This, My child, is your fresh start! Take ownership of your pain by placing it in My hands. I am the Lord your God, and I rule over all the world and over your life. Believe and receive. My love for you is greater than you could ever imagine, and I desire so much more for you than you could ever comprehend. But you must make a choice today to lay down your concerns and seek Me first.

Psalm 55:22; Psalm 121:2–4; 2 Chronicles 16:9; Isaiah 55:3, 6; Psalm 34:8; Joel 2:13; Matthew 21:22; Matthew 6:33

God's Promises

I, the Lord your God, will hold your right hand, saying to you, "Fear not, I will help you." (Isa. 41:13)

I will take you as My people, and I will be your God. Then you shall know that I am the Lord your God who brings you out from under the burdens of the Egyptians. (Exod. 6:7)

I will lift up my eyes to the hills—from whence comes my help? My help comes from the Lord, who made heaven and earth. He will not allow your foot to be moved; He who keeps you will not slumber. Behold, He who keeps Israel shall neither slumber nor sleep. (Ps. 121:1–4)

My Prayer

Heavenly Father, thank You for being Lord over all creation and Lord over my life. In these days of global and personal distress, I lift up my eyes to the hills. Where does my help come from? It comes from You, oh God, who made heaven and earth. You will not allow my foot to be moved. You will not slumber or sleep. You, Lord, are my keeper. You are my shade in the heat and my protection at night. You will preserve me from all evil and safeguard my soul. You will protect my going out and my coming in from this time and forevermore. Thank You for being my helper, my keeper, and my preserver. I yield myself to You in unwavering trust, knowing that You will strengthen my heart for such a time as this. I don't know what to do, but I will keep my eyes on You and trust that You will be faithful to me during this time of trouble and uncertainty. I commit myself to Your lordship. I will love You this day and every day with all my heart, soul, strength, and mind. Thank You, Lord, that through obedience to Your Word and Your all-sufficient grace I am made strong. Fill my cup, Lord, to overflowing, and fill my heart with Your heavenly song. In Jesus' name I pray. Amen.

Psalm 121:1–8; Lamentations 3:21–23

My Worship

Under His wings I am safely abiding.
Though the night deepens and tempests are wild,
Still I can trust Him; I know He will keep me.
He has redeemed me, and I am His child.

Under His wings, under His wings,
Who from His love can sever?
Under His wings my soul shall abide, safely abide forever.

Under His wings, what a refuge in sorrow!
How the heart yearningly turns to His rest!
Often when earth has no balm for my healing,
There I find comfort, and there I am blest.

Under His wings, O what precious enjoyment!
There will I hide till life's trials are o'er;
Sheltered, protected, no evil can harm me.
Resting in Jesus, I'm safe evermore.[35]

Reflection and Realignment

What disturbance in the world around you is weighing on your heart? Following and obeying God means submitting to Him as Lord, even when things seem out of control and darkness seems to get the upper hand. How might God be impressing upon your heart to submit your concerns to Him? Follow His leading, and then determine to pray deliberately over those things that trouble you. Read and meditate on Psalm 121.

DAY 36

I AM
Your Faithful Father

This prolonged time of weakness and discouragement has lasted for many months. You feel as if you can't take any more. Yet I know your frame, and I know how much you can take. I am your faithful Father, and I will help you and see you through. You are My child, so walk with confidence and receive the resources I have to help you. When you cry out, "Abba, Father," I will hear you and provide for you. As your divine Daddy, I am deeply concerned about all you are going through. My Spirit bears witness with your spirit that you are My child and heir, joint heir with My Son, Jesus Christ. In this time of affliction, you can trust Me, regardless of what is happening within you or around you, for I am fully trustworthy.

When you suffer, you do not suffer alone. I suffer with you. Intertwined like a three-strand cord, we are connected, and through your suffering you will experience a depth and richness of My glory that will see you through. Although at times life feels unbearable to you, in reality I am bearing the full weight of your load. "My yoke is easy and My burden is light." I am gentle with you, so be gentle with yourself. Give yourself permission to climb up onto My lap and rest your head on My shoulder.

I am here for you, My child, and I will not allow the undertow of confusing hardships to pull you down into a deep pit of despair. Even when your faith falters, you can find peace in Me. In this world you will have trouble, but take heart, for I have overcome the world.

Oh dear and precious child, I am so much closer to you than you think, and your suffering is not in vain. It is actually producing for you a depth of intimacy with Me that cannot be attained any other way. Depend upon Me, and trust Me to sustain you. Although bad things happen, I am in control. I can turn your mess into a masterpiece and your disaster into a great destiny. But you have a choice to make: will you trust Me, or will you allow your dejection to deter you from My divine plan?

The adversity you are now experiencing has clouded your perspective. But as I have encouraged you before, your difficulty has a purpose. In moments of dread, depend upon Me, your Father. I will sustain you, and you will not be moved. I keep My covenant and supply mercy for a thousand generations to those who love and obey Me. I do not change like shifting shadows, but I remain fully committed to you. In Me you will find rest. I will never leave you or forsake you.

View your time of suffering and adversity as a great garden of growth. Through this time I am growing in you a rich and vibrant faith that will stand strong even in times of drought or storm. I have allowed these obstacles into your life to teach you to depend wholeheartedly upon Me as you come to understand My father heart toward you. I desire to build perseverance into your character that will make you mature and complete, not lacking anything. But in order to keep the ground of your soul fertile, you must guard your heart from bitterness and self-pity. These obstacles will impede your growth and prevent you from flourishing. When these feelings come, instead of fueling them with thoughts of hurt and hostility, quench them with prayer and praise. By looking for My presence in the midst of your struggles, you will begin to thrive. Although the darkness consumes you, keep your eyes on My light, and behold the hidden treasures I have waiting for you.

Psalm 103:13–14; Romans 8:15; Philippians 4:19; Deuteronomy 32:4; Romans 8:16–17; Matthew 11:30; John 16:33; Philippians 3:8–10; 2 Corinthians 4:8–9; Psalm 16:8; Deuteronomy 7:9; James 1:17; 2 Timothy 2:13; Matthew 11:28; Deuteronomy 31:6; James 1:2–4

God's Promises

Behold what manner of love the Father has bestowed on us, that we should be called children of God! (1 John 3:1)

You did not receive the spirit of bondage again to fear, but you received the Spirit of adoption by whom we cry out, "Abba, Father." The Spirit Himself bears witness with our spirit that we are children of God, and if children, then heirs—heirs of God and joint heirs with Christ, if indeed we suffer with Him, that we may also be glorified together. For I consider that the sufferings of this present time are not worthy to be compared with the glory which shall be revealed in us. (Rom. 8:15–18)

May our Lord Jesus Christ Himself, and our God and Father, who has loved us and given us everlasting consolation and good hope by grace, comfort your hearts and establish you in every good word and work. (2 Thess. 2:16–17)

Every good gift and every perfect gift is from above, and comes down from the Father of lights, with whom there is no variation or shadow of turning. (James 1:17)

My Prayer

Faithful Father, please forgive me for losing sight of who You are. You are my Father, and I can rest in Your tender care for me as Your child. When difficulties arise, You are with me, and this battle I am fighting is not mine but Yours. Though this season I am walking through feels unbearable, give me the ability to stand on Your promises and remain strong in You. Oh, how my soul thirsts for You and my flesh longs for You in this dry and weary land. Replenish me now, oh God, by Your Spirit, and revive me once again with Your Word. Since Your loving-kindness is better than life, my lips will praise You. In this moment I lift up my hands and say, "Thank You for all You have done and all You are going to do, even through my adversity." As my faithful Father, You will see me through. Give me the courage to stand strong when I feel weak, the ability to persevere when I am ready to give up, and the patience to wait on You to work all things out for good. Thank You for being my divine Daddy who loves me without limit and cares for my every concern. I can fully depend upon You, even through these troubling times. In Jesus' name I pray. Amen.

2 Chronicles 20:15; Ephesians 6:10;
Psalm 63:1, 3; Romans 8:28

My Worship

O take my hand, dear Father, and lead Thou me,
Till at my journey's ending I dwell with Thee.
Alone I cannot wander one single day,
So do Thou guide my footsteps on life's rough way.

O cover with Thy mercy my poor, weak heart,
Lest I in joy or sorrow from Thee depart.
Permit Thy child to linger here at Thy feet,
Thy goodness blindly trusting with faith complete.

Though oft Thy power but faintly may stir my soul,
With Thee, my light in darkness, I reach the goal.
Take then my hand, dear Father, and lead Thou me,
Till at my journey's ending I dwell with Thee.[36]

Reflection and Realignment

Sometimes our trials drag on for so long that we think we can't take any more. But our desperation can lead us to finally turn to the One who can lift us up—our Father who wants us to give all our pain over to Him. Think of a time when you encountered a trial that felt unbearable. How long did it last? How did God reveal His fatherly love and care to you through that time? What did God teach you in that time that can help you through the adversity you are facing now? Write out a prayer asking God for a deeper understanding of His fatherly love and care for you through your present difficulty, and ask Him to help you see your tough time through His light-filled lens.

DAY 37

I AM
Your Potter

As you lie here pondering your upbringing, you feel marred and useless. You look into the mirror and see only your imperfections. The deep scars of your soul, though invisible, carry tremendous power as they deter you from embracing your full potential. Imprisoned by painful past experiences, you see them as hindrances to growth and purpose. But I see hope! I have created you with unlimited potential, and nothing can ever take that away. I am the potter, and you are the clay. Your imperfections can be reshaped in My hands.

As the master potter, I am creating you into My greatest work of art. You are the radiant fulfillment of My handiwork, My one-of-a-kind creation. Like a rare and precious jewel, you are being formed for My specific purpose and use. Even though you may be impaired, disfigured, or blemished, I will never toss you aside. I will patiently reshape you over and over again until you are flawless. I see your imperfections as part of a bigger picture than you do, and I see your scars as part of a larger plan than you can imagine. As you surrender yourself to Me and submit all you are and have into My hands, I will restore you. I use everything—yes, everything—in your life to help mold you and make you more into My image.

Although you try to conceal your scars, I want to expose and refashion them for My use. As long as you live, you will find no limits to the extraordinary things I can do. Redemption is My greatest work! I take delight in reclaiming that which is broken, abused, flawed, and used by giving it a new purpose. Even in your weak and fragile state, I desire to use you to accomplish great things so My power can be manifested in and through your life. All your past failures, mistakes, sin, and shame have been nailed to the cross and covered by the precious blood of My Son, Jesus Christ. His death and resurrection are the profound evidence of My extravagant love for you. Because of who He is and what He has done, you can live from this day forward with a richer, fuller, more abundant life. No longer imprisoned, you have been set free!

Your skewed perception of yourself, however, has deterred you from embracing My will for you. Although you do not see it, the truth is, you are My masterpiece, created to do good works and fulfill a plan like no one else can. Every cell in your body is equipped to heal, and every hole in your heart is able to be mended. Allow My love to fill your hollow places and heal your deepest hurts. I have the power to make all things new—even you, My child. Nothing is too broken that I cannot fix it, and no one is too marred that I cannot restore him or her.

Let this truth sink down into the deepest recesses of your soul. You are a new creation, forgiven and free from condemnation; the old is gone, and the new has come. Walk with confidence, and let My joy put a bounce in your step. A new beginning is about to burst forth—a new beginning just for you! "They shall rebuild the old ruins, they shall raise up the former desolations, and they shall repair the ruined cities, the desolations of many generations. . . . Instead of your shame you shall have double honor, and instead of confusion they shall rejoice in their portion. Therefore in their land they shall possess double; everlasting joy shall be theirs."

I Am Your Potter

Isaiah 64:8; John 10:10; Ephesians 2:10; Revelation 21:5;
2 Corinthians 5:17; Isaiah 61:4–7

God's Promises

Now, O Lord, You are our Father; we are the clay, and You our potter; and all we are the work of Your hand. (Isa. 64:8)

We are His workmanship, created in Christ Jesus for good works, which God prepared beforehand that we should walk in them. (Eph. 2:10)

If anyone is in Christ, he is a new creation; old things have passed away; behold, all things have become new. (2 Cor. 5:17)

We have this treasure in earthen vessels, that the excellence of the power may be of God and not of us. (2 Cor. 4:7)

He who sat on the throne said, "Behold, I make all things new." And He said to me, "Write, for these words are true and faithful." (Rev. 21:5)

My Prayer

Heavenly Father, my potter, forgive me for denying You access to every area of my life. I am clay, and in order for You to mold me, I must fully submit to You. But I have not fully surrendered and so have remained imprisoned by my past. Forgive me, Lord, and take charge of those areas of my life that I have withheld from You. Reshape them, and remake them fit for Your use. I praise You, oh God, that You make all things new. I claim Your promise from the book of Isaiah that instead of shame, You will give me double honor, and instead of confusion I will rejoice in my portion. Lord, I receive this promise in the deepest recesses of my heart and reject the lies. As I do, I embrace the truth of Your Word. I am a new creation in Christ; the old is gone, and the new has come. From this day forward I will live as a new creation. Thank You, God, for making me new. Thank You for releasing me from shame. Thank You for giving me a new heart, a fresh start, and a living hope through the resurrection of Jesus Christ. You can use anything from my past. Even the deepest wounds of my soul are repairable in Your almighty hands. Thank You, Lord! Though doubts still consume me at times, I tell my soul to say, "I trust You, God." Because You are my potter, I ask You to mold me and use all that I am and have for Your glory. Thank You for being a God of second chances and extending Your great love to me today. In Jesus' name I pray. Amen.

Isaiah 61:7; 2 Corinthians 5:17; 1 Peter 1:3

My Worship

Have Thine own way, Lord! Have Thine own way!
Thou art the potter, I am the clay.
Mold me and make me after Thy will,
while I am waiting, yielded and still.

Have Thine own way, Lord! Have Thine own way!
  Search me and try me, Savior today!
Wash me just now, Lord, wash me just now,
  as in Thy presence humbly I bow.

Have Thine own way, Lord! Have Thine own way!
  Wounded and weary, help me, I pray!
Power, all power, surely is Thine!
  Touch me and heal me, Savior divine!

Have Thine own way, Lord! Have Thine own way!
  Hold o'er my being absolute sway.
Fill with Thy Spirit till all shall see
  Christ only, always, living in me![37]

REFLECTION AND REALIGNMENT

How might God be reshaping you and refashioning the broken pieces and places in your life for His use? Those very things that you see as flaws may just be the foundation that God uses to reveal His power and strength in and through you. Take a moment to write out one of today's Scripture promises that has encouraged you, and claim it in a prayer, asking God to show you how He is molding you to make a difference and how you can join Him in the process.

DAY 38

I AM
He Who Is Able

I see that you are tired. Your journey has been long and the uphill climb strenuous. But I, your God, am He who is able to do exceedingly abundantly above all that you ask or think, according to the power that works in you. Come sit with Me, My child, and receive My whispers of love. While your ability is limited, I am able to transform your difficulty into something beautiful.

As the God who is able, I can "guide you continually, and satisfy your soul in drought, and strengthen your bones; you shall be like a watered garden, and like a spring of water, whose waters do not fail." I can speak peace to your heart. I can give you rest. Though your next step is uncertain, My presence will be with you, and I will keep your steps firm. But you must remain close to Me and trust Me to be your continual guide as the currents of My love carry you through this volatile time.

Often My ways do not make sense to you. When I guide, I guide you to where I want you to go, not always where you want to be. As you lean on Me, pressing in with prayer, I will make My desires your own. As you surrender your wants for My ways, you will receive deep and lasting satisfaction. You must fully trust Me, even though trusting is not easy for you, since others have broken your trust in the past. This is where I want to grow you. I want to strengthen your trust muscles. The sooner you can fully depend on Me, the sooner you will be set free from trying to figure out your future and fix your past. Only I know your future and can mend that which is broken in your past.

Like an underground spring that replenishes the stream above it, I am able to refresh your weary soul. Do not be like the Israelites, who had My full resources available to them yet turned aside to worthless substitutes—broken cisterns that held no water. I am the fountain of living water, and I never run dry. When I give, I give more than enough. Trust Me, My child, and do not lean on your own understanding. It is far better to lean on Me.

There are no quick solutions, however. I could certainly snap My fingers and make everything right, but that would not push you to pursue Me. There is a process to My plan, and your patience with the process is key. As you wait for Me, perseverance will be produced in your life that will enable you to shine. So do not give up. Stay diligent to the very end. From this day forward, let it be enough to know that when you think you can't—I can!

Ephesians 3:20; Isaiah 58:11; Matthew 11:28; Exodus 33:14; Psalm 37:23; Jeremiah 2:13; Psalm 107:9; Proverbs 3:5; James 1:12; Hebrews 6:11

God's Promises

God is able to make all grace abound toward you, that you, always having all sufficiency in all things, may have an abundance for every good work. (2 Cor. 9:8)

Ah, Lord God! Behold, You have made the heavens and the earth by Your great power and outstretched arm. There is nothing too hard for You. (Jer. 32:17)

To Him who is able to do exceedingly abundantly above all that we ask or think, according to the power that works in us, to Him be glory in the church by Christ Jesus to all generations, forever and ever. Amen. (Eph. 3:20–21)

My Prayer

Heavenly Father, I praise You today for being a God who is able! Though my heart is unsettled in the midst of uncertain times, I can fully trust You. You are greater than my needs, and You are able to turn my situation around. I give You all my apprehensions, cares, concerns, and questions, and I rest in Your goodness and Your love. In You I find my strength, and in You I find my hope. Nothing is too difficult for You, oh God, and nothing is beyond Your infinite reach. Your Word says that You can do exceedingly abundantly above all that we ask or think, according to Your power that works in us, and I believe this and claim it over my life. Increase my faith, oh God, to receive all that You have for me. Whether You turn my circumstances around or not, I want to live on higher ground. I want to rise above my challenges by having full assurance and trust in You, knowing that whatever happens will be according to Your perfect will and plan and can be used for my good and Your glory. In Jesus' name I pray. Amen.

Jeremiah 32:17; Ephesians 3:20; Romans 8:28

My Worship

I'm pressing on the upward way;
New heights I'm gaining every day,
Still praying as I'm onward bound,
"Lord, plant my feet on higher ground."

Lord, lift me up and let me stand
By faith on heaven's tableland.
A higher plane than I have found—
Lord, plant my feet on higher ground.

My heart has no desire to stay
Where doubts arise and fears dismay.
Though some may dwell where these abound,
My prayer, my aim, is higher ground.

I want to live above the world,
Though Satan's darts at me are hurled;
For faith has caught the joyful sound,
The song of saints on higher ground.

I want to scale the utmost height
And catch a gleam of glory bright;
But still I'll pray till heaven I've found,
"Lord, lead me on to higher ground."[38]

Reflection and Realignment

Remembering that God is able and all powerful is not easy, especially when we are faced with severe or uncertain hardships. In what area of your life is God calling you to trust Him more? Write it down, then write next to it, "Lord, today I rise above my challenges by trusting You with _____, because You are able to do far more than I imagine." Put today's date next to it, and select one of God's promises from today's devotional reading to claim over your need.

DAY 39

I AM
Your Exceedingly Great Reward

As you journey down the winding road toward healing and wholeness, I will call you to step out of your comfort zone into new and fuller service from Me. Along the way, however, you will encounter people who will not understand you or fathom why you do what you do. They may judge you, mock you, and even speak ill against you, but this is not your problem. Your responsibility is to continue to obey Me no matter what others say or do. Obedience to Me is costly, but it is well worth it! So whatever you do, do wholeheartedly for Me, for I am the giver of your reward, and not only that, but *I Myself* am your exceedingly great reward.

Whoever acknowledges My Son, Jesus Christ, before others I also will acknowledge that person. This is all you need to know. The proof I give you is in My Word, and that is more than enough. So do not merely listen to My Word, but do what it says. Believe it, and receive it as done. Walk in obedience to it, and you will remain in My love, prospering and bearing fruit that will last.

Let My pleasure wash over you and drain away your cares and concerns. It really does not matter what others think. Their faulty perceptions fall short of My loving thoughts toward you. You are My child, and I rejoice over you. No one can take that away— *no one.* Stand firm and be courageous. Let nothing move you. Always give yourself to serving Me wholeheartedly, and rich will be your reward.

Keep your eyes keenly fixed upon Me, and fight for your faith. Protect it! Do not let your enthusiasm die or your zeal fizzle out, for behold, at the proper time I will deal with all those who afflict you. I will also give you praise and fame in every land where you have been put to shame. Live fearlessly, not as one stifled under the heat of humiliation but rather as one strengthened for service under My protective armor. I have already taken away your judgments and cast out the enemy before you. I, the King of Israel, the Lord, am with you, and I am mighty.

Colossians 3:23–24; Genesis 15:1; Matthew 10:32; James 1:22;
Mark 11:24; Deuteronomy 5:33; John 15:16; Zephaniah 3:17;
1 Corinthians 15:58; Zephaniah 3:19; Ephesians 6:10–11; Zephaniah 3:15

God's Promises

The word of the Lord came to Abram in a vision, saying, "Do not be afraid, Abram. I am your shield, your exceedingly great reward." (Gen. 15:1)

The Lord repay your work, and a full reward be given you by the Lord God of Israel, under whose wings you have come for refuge. (Ruth 2:12)

Whatever you do, do it heartily, as to the Lord and not to men, knowing that from the Lord you will receive the reward of the inheritance; for you serve the Lord Christ. (Col. 3:23–24)

He who comes to God must believe that He is, and that He is a rewarder of those who diligently seek Him. (Heb. 11:6)

Be steadfast, immovable, always abounding in the work of the Lord, knowing that your labor is not in vain in the Lord. (1 Cor. 15:58)

My Prayer

Heavenly Father, thank You for being both my rewarder and my exceedingly great reward. There is none like You, oh God. None! You alone are worthy of my praise. Even though I pass through the waters, You are with me, and as I pass through the rivers, I will not drown. The fire and the flames will not overtake me, for You, oh God, are with me and will keep me safe in Your hand. Help me, Lord, to live fearlessly and to abandon myself to obeying You no matter the cost. If You are for me, who can be against me? You are my greatest ally, aid, and advocate. But I must confess that I am struggling as I consider the sacrifice involved in stepping out of my comfort zone and into the unknown. I realize, Lord, that even those I love and care about may not understand. This is where I need to trust You. Your love, oh God, is higher than the heavens, and Your faithfulness reaches to the skies. As I reflect on You and Your awesome powers, I am undone. Apart from You I can do nothing, but with You I can do all things.

Thank You for giving meaning to my life. In You I have purpose.
In You I have hope. In Jesus' name I pray. Amen.

Isaiah 43:2–3; Romans 8:31; Psalm 108:4; John 15:5; Philippians 4:13

My Worship

When we walk with the Lord
In the light of His Word,
What a glory He sheds on our way!
While we do His good will,
He abides with us still
And with all who will trust and obey.

Trust and obey, for there's no other way
To be happy in Jesus but to trust and obey.

Not a shadow can rise,
Not a cloud in the skies,
But His smile quickly drives it away.
Not a doubt or a fear,
Not a sigh or a tear
Can abide while we trust and obey.

Not a burden we bear,
Not a sorrow we share,
But our toil He doth richly repay;
Not a grief or a loss,
Not a frown or a cross,
But is blest if we trust and obey.

But we never can prove
The delights of His love
Until all on the altar we lay;
For the favor He shows,
And the joy He bestows,
Are for them who will trust and obey.

Then in fellowship sweet
We will sit at His feet,
Or we'll walk by His side in the way.
What He says we will do;
Where He sends we will go;
Never fear, only trust and obey.[39]

Reflection and Realignment

Obeying the Lord can be costly, as it often requires stepping out of our comfort zones and into something foreign or unknown. Our obedience may also be misunderstood by those close to us. In what area of your life is God prompting you to obey Him? Maybe you are fearful because of a bad past experience, the adjustment it would require, what others may think, or your fear that you are ill equipped or inept. As you encounter this crossroads, write down your fears involved with obeying. Next to each fear write down one of God's promises to counteract that fear. Then pray, asking the Lord to give you courage to obey Him and the ability to accept His reward rather than the approval and acceptance of others. The cost is worth the reward!

DAY 40

I AM
Your King of Glory

The worries and concerns of life will always seek to distract you from Me. But as you learn to dismiss them, you will discover the greatest gift: My glory. Look outside and see the grass, the flowers, the trees, and the birds. All creation manifests My glory just by being what I created it to be. I, your King of glory, want you also to be who I created you to be, nothing more, nothing less—even if that means just being the best wife and mom you can be in your low-functioning, exhausted state. As you are, My glory will shine through you.

As you bask in My glory, forgetting about yourself and resting in Me, I will give you comfort and hope to keep on keeping on and not to give in to discouragement in the physical and spiritual battles you will experience. Instead, My glory—My powerful presence—will radiate through you as the sunshine radiates through a room on a bright morning. I am greater than your struggle. My strength will not fizzle out but will remain steadfast for you in battle.

Even in the doldrums of your mundane experiences, adventure awaits you. I am preparing you for something new—something beyond what you could ever achieve or accomplish on your own. This is so the world will see Me through you and know that I AM. But for this to unfold, My glory must shine in your life!

I am strong and mighty, and My plans for you will prevail. Any time you face difficulties or the uncertainties of this life overwhelm you, just remember who I am and to whom you belong. I am the King of glory, the Most High, who reigns over your valleys as well as your victories. I am unstoppable, immovable, unchangeable, uncontainable, and My love for you never ends. As you turn your eyes from your weakness to My glory, My power will rise within you. Clothed with honor and majesty, I unfold the heavens like a curtain. If I can do all this, how much more can I untangle the troubles of your life?

The difficulties of your days are nothing compared to My divine enabling within you. For "as your days, so shall your strength be." Trust Me, My child. I am King! No problem is too big for Me to handle. I am greater than your greatest difficulty and stronger than your strongest foe. From the mountaintops to the valleys, I AM.

This is your turning point. No longer do you need to look at your situation as a huge mountain that cannot be moved. Fix your gaze on Me and My glory, and your troubles will be minimized and your soul comforted. This is the gift you will receive as you take the time to switch your focus from your troubles to My presence.

It is time for you to fully embrace your blessing—the blessing of My glory—the blessing of Me. I am with you, and I am sending you. Do not be afraid; I am your all in all. Look at Me, and let My glory shine!

Psalm 24:8; Psalm 83:18; Psalm 104:1–2; Deuteronomy 33:25;
Psalm 73:23–24; Isaiah 48:16–17

God's Promises

Who is this King of glory? The LORD strong and mighty, the LORD mighty in battle. (Ps. 24:8)

The Word became flesh and dwelt among us, and we beheld His glory, the glory as of the only begotten of the Father, full of grace and truth. (John 1:14)

We all, with unveiled face, beholding as in a mirror the glory of the Lord, are being transformed into the same image from glory to glory, just as by the Spirit of the Lord. (2 Cor. 3:18)

Jesus said to her, "Did I not say to you that if you would believe you would see the glory of God?" (John 11:40)

May the God of all grace, who called us to His eternal glory by Christ Jesus, after you have suffered a while, perfect, establish, strengthen, and settle you. To Him be the glory and dominion forever and ever. Amen. (1 Pet. 5:10)

My Prayer

Heavenly Father, my precious and powerful King of glory, I praise Your name today, for You are ever so great. At times I have lost sight of Your majesty and allowed my anxieties to consume and distract me from Your glory. Thank You for Your promised forgiveness. There is none like You, oh God. No one else can resolve the problems I face, but You have the power to redeem them all. From the smallest uncertainty to the largest obstacle, You are able. Today I rest on Your promises, knowing that You can and will use my troubling times for my good and Your glory. I am not seeing all the good right now, but I believe it will come. I say yes to everything You have prepared for me. Help me live my life to the fullest as I completely rely on You—and You alone! In Jesus' name I pray. Amen.

1 John 1:9; Revelation 21:5; Ephesians 3:20; Romans 8:28

My Worship

Come, Thou Almighty King;
Help us Thy name to sing.
Help us to praise.
Father all glorious, o'er all victorious,
Come and reign over us,
Ancient of days.

Come, Thou incarnate Word,
Gird on Thy mighty sword.
Our prayer attend.
Come, and Thy people bless,
And give Thy Word success.
Spirit of holiness,
On us descend.

Come, holy comforter,
Thy sacred witness bear
In this glad hour.
Thou, who almighty art,

> Now rule in every heart
> And ne'er from us depart,
> Spirit of pow'r.
>
> To Thee, great One in Three,
> Eternal praises be
> Hence evermore.
> Thy sovereign majesty
> May we in glory see,
> And to eternity
> Love and adore.[40]

REFLECTION AND REALIGNMENT

God can take the worst problems and turn them around for good to accomplish His purposes in our lives (see Rom. 8:28). Consider a difficulty you are currently experiencing. Where is your focus as you wait for it to pass—on the problem or on God and His glory? Put your focus fully on God, and ask Him to show you His perspective on your concerns and help you experience His love in them. As He does, His presence within you will shine, and you will radiate peace. "This I recall to my mind, therefore I have hope. Through the LORD's mercies we are not consumed, because His compassions fail not. They are new every morning; great is Your faithfulness" (Lam. 3:21–23).

In My Grip

Sometimes life seems so uncertain,
the path ahead unclear.
But in these times we're not forgotten,
God goes before us and is near.

Fainting and faltering, our weaknesses rise,
casting doubt and darkening our view.
But God's promises are certain; He is with us,
And He will surely see us through.

His faithfulness, our foundation.
His Word, our guiding light.
His presence, our protection.
His love, our delight.

He will lead us and guide us
from this point to the next.
He says, "Trust Me, child, and follow.
I will carry you through this test.

No need to worry, My child.
I am the author of your life and plan.
The path before you is certain with Me,
your guide, your Redeemer, your friend.

No darkness will deter My desire
to bring good from each struggle and pain.
The purpose I have in this trial
will bring greater glory to My holy name.

So rest in My care and provisions;
You are safe in My infinite grip.
The journey before you is marked by My hand,
and I will not let you slip."[41]

About the Author

Sonya Grace Naugle is just an ordinary girl with a God-given purpose to encourage individuals through their hardships with a message of faith, hope, and love. Having endured her own heartache from a broken, wounded childhood and a chronic health condition, Sonya has learned firsthand to trust God and hear His voice through life's hard places.

As a speaker and writer, Sonya comes alongside individuals struggling through all walks and seasons of life and provides them encouragement from the comfort she has received from God through her own life's struggles (see 2 Cor. 1:3–4). Sonya is a dedicated wife, mother of four, and grandmother of two. She is also a registered nurse, having earned her degree from Alvernia University. Sonya has a bachelor of science in Bible from Lancaster Bible College. Combining her education with a heart of compassion and a hand of tender mercy, Sonya serves alongside her husband, Nathanael, in full-time pastoral ministry to provide help and hope for individuals and families within their congregation and community nestled in the rolling hills of southeastern Pennsylvania.

Pronunciation Guide and Meanings for the Names of God

Adonai (ah-do-NAI)—Lord, Master
Elohim (e-lo-HEEM)—all-powerful Creator
El (el)—the strong One
El Elohei Yisra'el (el el-o-HAY yis-raw-EL)—the God of Israel
El Elyon (el el-YOHN)—the God Most High
El Olam (el o-LAM)—the eternal, everlasting God
El Ro'i (el ro-I)—the God who sees me
El Shaddai (el shad-DAI)—God Almighty, all-sufficient One
Machaseh (mach-a-SEH)—refuge
Ma'on (ma-OHN)—dwelling place
Yahweh (yah-WEH), or Jehovah (yeh-ho-VAH)—the proper name of the God of Israel; I AM, the Lord
Yahweh Mekaddishchem (yah-WEH mek-KAH-dish-KEM)—the Lord who sanctifies you
Yahweh Nissi (yah-WEH nis-SEE)—the Lord my banner
Yahweh Ra'ah (yah-WEH rah-AH)—the Lord my shepherd

Yahweh Rapha (yah-WEH ra-FA)—the Lord who heals
Yahweh Shalom (yah-WEH sha-LOME)—the Lord is peace
Yahweh Shammah (yah-WEH sham-MAH)—the Lord is there
Yahweh Tzeva'ot (yah-WEH tze-va-OAT)—the Lord of hosts
Yahweh Tzidkenu (yah-WEH tzid-KAY-nu)—the Lord my righteousness
Yahweh Tzur (yah-WEH tzur)—the Lord my rock
Yahweh Yir'eh (yah-WEH yir-EH)—the Lord will provide

OTES

1. Joachim Neander, "Praise to the Lord, the Almighty," 1680.
2. Joseph H. Gilmore, "He Leadeth Me," 1862.
3. Isaac Watts, "I Sing the Mighty Power of God," 1715.
4. Katharina von Schlegel, "Be Still, My Soul," 1752.
5. Civilla D. Martin, "God Will Take Care of You," 1904.
6. Sonya Grace Naugle, "Living Water," 2011.
7. Mary E. Byrne, trans., "Be Thou My Vision," 1905.
8. Frederick M. Lehman, "The Love of God," 1917.
9. Naugle, "Today," 2011.
10. Isaac Watts, "O God, Our Help in Ages Past," 1719.
11. Clara H. Scott, "Open My Eyes, That I May See," 1895.
12. Eliza Edmunds Hewitt, "Fear Not, I Am with Thee," 1898.
13. Martin Luther, "A Mighty Fortress Is Our God," 1529; trans. Frederick H. Hedge, 1852.
14. Attr. Dorothy A. Thrupp, "Savior, Like a Shepherd Lead Us," 1836.
15. Kate Ulmer, "Step by Step," 1922.
16. George Matheson, "O Love That Will Not Let Me Go," 1882.
17. Frances R. Havergal, "Like a River Glorious," 1874.
18. Naugle, "God of Compassion," 2011.
19. Robert Robinson, "Come, Thou Fount of Every Blessing," 1758.
20. Augustus M. Toplady, "Rock of Ages," 1776.
21. Fanny J. Crosby, "Redeemed," 1882.
22. Charles Wesley, "And Can It Be," 1738.
23. Naugle, "Through the Storm," 2011.
24. Benjamin M. Ramsey, "Teach Me Thy Way, O Lord," 1919.
25. Caroline V. Sandell-Berg, "Day by Day," 1865.

26. Crosby, "Falter Not," 1891.
27. Sarepta M. I. Henry, "My Father Knows," 1897.
28. Edward Mote, "The Solid Rock," 1834.
29. Anna L. Waring, "In Heavenly Love Abiding," 1850.
30. Naugle, "I Am Yours, Lord," 2011.
31. Crosby, "Come, Great Deliverer, Come," 1877.
32. William W. Walford, "Sweet Hour of Prayer," 1845.
33. Naugle, "We Have Seen Your Glory," 2011.
34. Horatio G. Spafford, "It Is Well with My Soul," 1873.
35. William O. Cushing, "Under His Wings," 1896.
36. Julie K. von Hausmann, "Oh Take My Hand, Dear Father," 1862.
37. Adelaide A. Pollard, "Have Thine Own Way, Lord," 1906.
38. Johnson Oatman Jr., "Higher Ground," 1898.
39. John H. Sammis, "Trust and Obey," 1887.
40. Attr. Wesley, "Come, Thou Almighty King," 1757.
41. Naugle, "In My Grip," 2016.

Selected Bibliography

Names of God: 21 Names of God and Their Meanings. Torrance, CA: Rose, 2003.

Sing to the Lord Hymnal. Kansas City, MI: Lillenas, 1993.

Spangler, Ann. *Praying the Names of God: A Daily Guide.* Grand Rapids: Zondervan, 2004.

Unger, Merrill F. *Unger's Bible Dictionary.* Chicago: Moody, 1979.

Made in the USA
Coppell, TX
15 April 2020